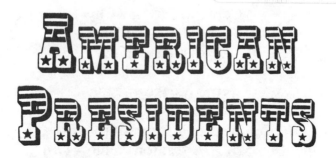

AMERICAN PRESIDENTS

Fascinating Facts, Stories, & Questions of Our Chief Executives And Their Families

by Richard L. McElroy
(with illustrations by Walt Neal)

To Harold —
I hope you enjoy my book! & All Best Wishes - Good reading
R.L. McElroy
Psalm 139
12/1/96

Daring Books
Canton • Ohio

ISBN 0-938936-18-2

For further information, write
Box 526 AP, Canton, Ohio 44701

Cover Photo:
An exhibit sponsored by
THE NATIONWIDE INSURANCE
ORGANIZATION
at
THE CENTER OF SCIENCE AND INDUSTRY
Columbus, Ohio
*A place with things you can't discover
anywhere else!*
Used with permission.

Photographer: Nancy Black, The Dixie Studio

Library of Congress Cataloging in Publication Data

McElroy, Richard L., 1947—
    American presidents.

    Bibliography: p.
    1. Presidents--United States--Miscellanea.
    2. United States--Politics and government--Miscellanea.
    I. Title.
    E176.1.M426   1984   973 '.09 '92   84-9606
    ISBN 0-938936-18-2

Dedication

This book is dedicated to all of my students,
past and present, whom I have had the privilege
of serving in my classroom.

Foreword

Did you ever wonder how many Americans have wanted to be President of the United States? Certainly, the number is greater than the two or more persons whose names have appeared on the ballots as Presidential candidates of the major parties every four years since George Washington was named President by the Electoral College in 1789.

In the twentieth century, there have been such formidable third-party candidates as Theodore Roosevelt, the Progressive standard-bearer in 1912; Strom Thurmond, the States' Rights candidate in 1948; and John Anderson, the Independent in 1980. And in each election, there are many minor-party candidates (as many as three hundred), most of whom remain unknown.

In the nominating process, the major parties must consider the merits of many who are willing—even eager—to be the nation's Chief Executive. For example, in 1984, eight men sought the Democratic nomination. And, it is reasonable to assume that many Republicans would have tossed their hats into the ring had Ronald Reagan not been so firmly entrenched as an incumbent.

Many are called, but few are chosen. Only 40 men have reached the Presidency in our nation's history. Some Presidents, like Gerald Ford, Andrew Johnson, and Chester A. Arthur, have attained membership in this exclusive group only by happenstance. They were never elected by their fellow citizens.

Because of its exclusiveness there is little wonder that so many men have openly aspired to be members of this fraternity. Today, however, the nature of the fraternity may be on the verge of undergoing a drastic change, for it appears that the nation is increasingly willing to have a woman serve as its President. Goodness knows how many women in the past secretly yearned to lead the nation as its President, and how many women in the future will be willing to openly declare their ambitions to occupy the White House in a role other than as the First Lady.

But the future is conjecture; the past is fact. Presidential information lies within a mountain of literature. Most Americans pride themselves on their knowledge of the Presidents, and with only forty of them to concentrate on, we might assume the average person would be quite an expert. But can you name all of the Presidents—not necessarily in order? Can you place each of them in his proper historic era? Can you recall some of the achievements and failures of their administrations?

Rich McElroy can, but he has the advantage of being an astute scholar of the Presidency, as well as a social studies (we used to call it history) teacher. His wide range of activities and talents also include that of city councilman, amateur athlete, magazine editor and coach. Fortunately, his versatility and enthusiasm wells over into the classroom, where he challenges his students to get involved with their course work.

In this, his second book, he opens the classroom door for us, not in a pedagogic manner, but in an easy-going, fact-filled way. In it, you will encounter facts and stories you perhaps once knew but have forgotten and things that you never knew. Don't let that discourage you; this book will whet your appetite to learn more about the Presidents, to get reacquainted with them. And once it succeeds in doing that, it may serve as a springboard for further knowledge through reading.

Gene Winski

Acknowledgements

I wish to thank the following people for their assistance on this project: Bob Weible and cartoonist Walt Neal of Akron, Ruth Plaskett and Daryl Revoldt of North Canton, Al Simpson of Washington, D.C., Harold Thomas and Fred Doerfler of Canton, and the fine people at the Stark County District Library. In addition, materials were also provided by the Ohio Historical Society and the Smithsonian Institution. Also, I owe a debt of gratitude to my family, especially my wife, Pamela, whose patience and understanding made this work possible. And to my children, Matthew, Rachael and Luke for any time which was taken from them. Most of all, my thanks goes to Tom Hayes. His research, dedication, insight and friendly criticism made this book a labor of love for more than two years. Without him, this project would have been an impossibility.

Introduction

As a boy in Smithfield, Ohio, I was quite adventurous, constantly restless, and often repugnant. During one particular confrontation with my mother, she sent me to my room with a book on U.S. Presidents. Her victory was complete, yet short-lived. As I read the book I became fascinated with those historical figures who have guided our "ship of state" since the time of George Washington. I wanted to know more.

I can still recall watching President Eisenhower in 1955 on that somewhat new creation called television. As a junior high student, my studies of Ohio and American History allowed me a closer look and better understanding of these men, their families and their effects upon the course of events. Later, as a social studies teacher and writer, I learned even more. Eventually I began collecting books and visiting the homes of past Presidents.

No person in the world can really understand the Presidency except the man in the Oval Office. And no person today lives in a bigger "goldfish bowl" than the President of the United States. His every gesture, spoken word, and motives are carefully scrutinized, analyzed or criticized by the media. There is no private life for him or his family while he is in office. Often times the criticism of him is unfair or exaggerated.

Gerald Ford is a good example. Ford was one of our most athletic Chief Executives. An outstanding football player, he was also very good at skiing and tennis. But twice he tripped coming down the steps of an airplane, and soon the entire world saw pictures of the President stumbling in public. Comedians then began using the incident in their routines, grossly exaggerating and implying that Ford was not only uncoordinated, but "mentally clumsy" as well. As unfair as this was, Ford could not alter this image. And more than one of the President's advisors admitted that this "character assassination" was one of the reasons he lost the election to Jimmy Carter in 1976.

Every President has had, like us, flaws in his character or personality. The administrations of these men were often reflective of their disposition. Washington and John Adams were very formal, even "stuffy." Lincoln was a poor administrator, and Andrew Johnson was stubborn. Polk and Hayes might be considered humorless. Coolidge was non-communicative and Truman and Lyndon Johnson short-tempered. Others were strong in their leadership role; others were weak or too compromising. Some, like William Harrison, Taylor, Garfield and Kennedy did not get much of an opportunity to demonstrate their abilities due to the brevity and tragedy surrounding their terms in office.

All of our Presidents did what they felt was

in the best interests of their country. They all tried in their own way to do the job as they saw fit. With a few minor exceptions, their actions have demonstrated a generosity, concern, and benevolence uncommon in most nations of the free world.

We citizens of these fifty United States can be thankful that the men who occupied the White House were basically honest, well-meaning individuals. Our democratic form of government has not permitted any man to become a despot or cruel dictator. Even when he tried, a President rarely succeeded in overstepping his bounds within our system of checks and balances.

My work here is a look at the Presidents in human terms. Included are some amusing, and some not-so-funny incidents. There are also some questions and game-type activities concerning the Presidents and the First Families. If you have only a slight interest in this subject, it is my intent to generate more. And if you like to read and discover more about our U.S. Presidents, I hope you will find this book entertaining, interesting, satisfying, and challenging.

Presidents
of the United States

Name	Political Party	Term of Office
George Washington	Federalist	1789-1797
John Adams	Federalist	1797-1801
Thomas Jefferson	Dem-Republican	1801-1809
James Madison	Dem-Republican	1809-1817
James Monroe	Dem-Republican	1817-1825
John Quincy Adams	Dem-Republican	1825-1829
Andrew Jackson	Democrat	1829-1837
Martin Van Buren	Democrat	1837-1841
William H. Harrison	Whig	1841
John Tyler	Whig	1841-1845
James K. Polk	Democrat	1845-1849
Zachary Taylor	Whig	1849-1850
Millard Fillmore	Whig	1850-1853
Franklin Pierce	Democrat	1853-1857
James Buchanan	Democrat	1857-1861
Abraham Lincoln	Republican	1861-1865
Andrew Johnson	Democrat	1865-1869
Ulysses S. Grant	Republican	1869-1877
Rutherford B. Hayes	Republican	1877-1881
James A. Garfield	Republican	1881
Chester A. Arthur	Republican	1881-1885
Grover Cleveland	Democrat	1885-1889
Benjamin Harrison	Republican	1889-1893
Grover Cleveland	Democrat	1893-1897
William McKinley	Republican	1897-1901
Theodore Roosevelt	Republican	1901-1909
William H. Taft	Republican	1909-1913
Woodrow Wilson	Democrat	1913-1921
Warren G. Harding	Republican	1921-1923
Calvin Coolidge	Republican	1923-1929
Herbert Hoover	Republican	1929-1933
Franklin D. Roosevelt	Democrat	1933-1945
Harry S. Truman	Democrat	1945-1953
Dwight D. Eisenhower	Republican	1953-1961
John F. Kennedy	Democrat	1961-1963
Lyndon B. Johnson	Democrat	1963-1969
Richard M. Nixon	Republican	1969-1974
Gerald R. Ford	Republican	1974-1977
Jimmy Carter	Democrat	1977-1981
Ronald Reagan	Republican	1981-

Quiz Time

Answers begin on page 135.

1. Who was the first President born in a hospital?

2. So you think you know your horoscope. More U.S. Presidents have been born under this zodiac sign than any other. Which sign?

3. One Chief Executive made it known that he cared little for music. In fact, he once told a group of men, "I only know two tunes. One of them is 'Yankee Doodle' and the other one isn't." Who made this quote?

4. Which President kept his pet cow "Pauline" grazing on the White House lawn?

5. While on a hunting expedition in Maryland, this nation's leader once shot a pig, because he thought it was a raccoon. Who was this "keen-eyed" hunter?

6. Which President took his oath of office TWICE in a 24-hour period?

7. Who was the oldest man ever elected as President?

8. This President was the first to make a radio broadcast and the first to ride to his inauguration in a car. Name him.

9. What President's portrait is on the $1000 U.S. Savings Bond?

10. This Chief Executive was ambidextrous (could write with both hands at the same time), needed specially-made hats to fit his large head, and was also one of our country's youngest generals. Name him.

11. Who was the first President to have an airplane license?

12. Raised a reformed Protestant, this eleven-year-old boy (and later President) kissed the hand of the Pope. Name him.

13. Who was the first President to have his photograph taken?

14. Who was the first Chief Executive to be photographed with his entire cabinet?

15. As you may have read in number 5, a

President once shot a pig because he thought it was a raccoon. But what national leader once used tobacco as fishing bait, and cussed when a "big one" got away?

16. What TWO states have the nickname "Mother of Presidents"?

17. Which President got stuck in a White House bathtub and a theater seat?

18. Who was the last President born in a log cabin?

19. Which man, while serving as a U.S. Representative, was chosen as both a U.S. Senator and President at approximately the same time, but resigned his Senate seat to take his oath of office as President?

20. Who was the last Chief Executive to serve in the Civil War?

21. Four Presidents have been killed in office. Two of those four met their assassins face-to-face. Name them.

22. Here's an easy one. Has a First Lady ever died while her husband was in office?

23. One First Lady survived her husband more than 40 years after his term of office expired. Name her.

24. Which President lived the LEAST amount of time after leaving office?

25. Which man, while serving in the White House, was accused by political opponents of beating his wife?

26. Which President was the first whose life was threatened by an assassin?

27. Who was the first President to have both parents at his inauguration?

28. Match the nicknames with the respective Presidents in the right-hand column. You must match them all correctly to get number 28 correct.

A. Blood and Whiskers	1. Andrew Johnson
B. The Veto President	2. Grover Cleveland
C. Tippecanoe	3. James Madison
D. Old Rough and Ready	4. Andrew Jackson
E. The Little Magician	5. Martin Van Buren
F. Old Hickory	6. William Henry Harrison
G. Father of the Constitution	7. Zachary Taylor
H. Tennessee	8. Ulysses S. Grant

29. Which President once conducted a band before hundreds of thousands of people during his time in office?

30. True or False: The teddy bear was named after Theodore Roosevelt.

31. Which two Presidents publicly urged their future successors not to seek a third term?

32. Which future President was once told by his father, "It's a lucky thing you were not born a girl, because you can't say no!"?

33. What Vice President always addressed his chief as "Cap'n," even in private meetings?

34. Who was the first mother to witness the inauguration of her son?

35. This President managed to have a special bill passed in Congress so his absent Vice President could take his oath in Cuba. Name him.

36. Which President was referred to as "His Accidency" even by his own party leaders?

37. Match the following themes or nicknames of the various administrations with that of the respective leader. You must get all eleven matched correctly to count number 37 right.

A. The Great Society	1. Dwight D. Eisenhower
B. Middle Road	2. Woodrow Wilson
or New Crusade	3. Lyndon Johnson
C. The Square Deal	4. Harry Truman
D. The Fair Deal	5. Andrew Johnson
E. Manifest Destiny	6. James Polk
F. The New Frontier	7. John Kennedy
G. The New Deal	8. Franklin D. Roosevelt
H. Era of Good Feeling	9. Theodore Roosevelt
I. Age of Hate	10. James Monroe
J. Period of No Decision	11. Benjamin Harrison
K. The New Freedom	

38. True or False: Maxwell House Coffee's slogan "Good to the last drop" was invented by Theodore Roosevelt.

39. William H. Taft began the tradition of throwing out the first baseball to mark the beginning of each season. But Taft also introduced another idea that has become very much a part of the game. What was it?

40. Which President had the most children?

KISSING BABIES ALWAYS DID COME NATURAL TO ME!

41. Was it Reagan, Kennedy, Lincoln, Polk, or Monroe who said, "No President who performs his duty faithfully and conscientiously can have any leisure."?

42. Were any of our Chief Executives, while serving in the military, ever wounded in battle?

43. Who gave the longest inaugural address?

44. This man was the only one of our Chief Executives to study medicine, only to leave college to fight in a war. Name him.

45. Who was the youngest President to take office?

46. Which President had the youngest Vice President?

47. Who was the first President to have "Hail to the Chief" played for him?

48. Which President gave the shortest Inaugural Day speech?

49. Here's a tough one. Who was the first Chief of State to be dressed entirely in American clothes?

50. Since George Washington first took office, the United States has had only one

day when there was no President. When was this?

51. This is a tricky one. Which President had a daughter who married a future President?

52. What was significant or unique about the Presidential election of November 7, 1848?

53. He was called the "President without a Party" and all of his cabinet members, except one, resigned within six months. Name him.

54. What President's father was a signer of the Declaration of Independence?

55. Who was the only President who took part in two inaugural ceremonies in two different nation's capitals?

56. Let's see how well you know your Presidents. Match the following Vice Presidents with their bosses. If you get just seven of the eleven matched correctly, count this question as right.

A. Charles Fairbanks   1. James Monroe
B. Daniel Tompkins   2. Theodore Roosevelt
C. George Clinton   3. Grover Cleveland (2nd term)
D. Thomas Marshall   4. Richard Nixon
E. Adlai Stevenson, Sr.   5. Ulysses S. Grant
F. George Dallas   6. James Polk

G. Garret Hobart   7. William McKinley
H. Spiro Agnew   8. William H. Taft
I. James Sherman   9. Thomas Jefferson
J. Thomas Hendricks   10. Grover Cleveland (1st term)
K. Schuyler Colfax   11. Woodrow Wilson

57. Which President's dog tried to ride to the inaugural ceremonies, only to be repeatedly removed from the automobile?

58. Who was the only President born in the state of Nebraska?

59. Lyndon B. Johnson was born in Texas. So was one other President. Who was he?

60. What national leader got lost in the woods for two hours trying to find the nation's capital?

61. Who was the first President inaugurated in long pants?
62. What man served as President just one day?
63. Which President was sworn in by his cousin, who was also Chief Justice of the Supreme Court and a political opponent?
64. Who was the only Chief Executive born in Illinois?
65. What man was elected President even though his name was not on the ballot in at least ten states?
66. True or False: The most dangerous job in the United States is the Presidency.
67. Who was the first President to appoint a woman to his cabinet?
68. Which President, as a teenager, fell in love with one of his school teachers and married her?

I NOW PRONOUNCE YOU PRESIDENT AND FIRST LADY—

69. Two men, while serving in the White House, earned the Nobel Peace Prize. Name just one.

70. This President, born and raised in the South, was a staunch Unionist. He informed his "Dixie" friends, some of whom served in his cabinet, that he would personally lead an army if a rebellion began—and that he would hang rebels if captured. Name him.

71. Some Presidents were better known by their middle names, instead of their first names. Match the following men with their first names.

A. Woodrow Wilson   1. John
B. Grover Cleveland   2. Hiram
C. Calvin Coolidge   3. Stephen
D. Ulysses Grant   4. Thomas

72. What is the average life expectancy for the men serving as President?

73. Only one of our Presidents was born on the Fourth of July. Name him.

74. Which Chief Executive had his salary doubled from one year to the next?

75. Who was the first President to ride a train while serving in office?

24

76. Five Presidential families witnessed the death of a son or daughter during the White House years. Name three of them.

77. Two Presidents had sons who were awarded the Congressional Medal of Honor, the nation's highest military award. Name just one.

78. Which President made custom-tailored suits for a President?

79. Who was the first President to appoint a black man to a cabinet post?

80. Which President was the first one to cross the Atlantic while in office?

81. Which President took his oath of office on Wall Street in New York City?

82. Who is the only U.S. President to have a foreign capital named after him?

83. Which one of the following Chief Executives did *not* smoke cigars?
A) James Garfield
B) Ulysses Grant
C) John Kennedy
D) Woodrow Wilson

84. Only one First Lady had the first name of Dorothea. Who was she?
A) Eleanor Roosevelt
B) Lucy Hayes
C) Jackie Kennedy
D) Dolley Madison

85. Which American President refused an honorary degree from Oxford University in England?
A) John Tyler
B) Lyndon Johnson
C) Millard Fillmore
D)Chester Arthur

86. Who was the only President to have a child born in the White House?
A) John Kennedy
B) Thomas Jefferson
C) Grover Cleveland
D) James Monroe

87. Only two President-First Lady "teams" celebrated a silver wedding anniversary in the White House. Which one of the following did?
A) Rutherford and Lucy Hayes
B) Warren and Florence Harding
C) Abraham and Mary Lincoln
D) Ronald and Nancy Reagan

88. Only one Vice President (and later President) attended every cabinet meeting at his President's request. Name him.
A) Richard Nixon
B) Calvin Coolidge
C) Andrew Johnson
D) Theodore Roosevelt

89. Which one of the following is NOT a qualification for a man running for the Presidency?
A) He must be at least 35 years old.
B) He must be a natural born citizen of the U.S.
C) He must never have served time in jail.
D) He must have lived at least 14 years in the U.S.

90. Which one of the following men weighed the least as President?
A) James Monroe
B) William McKinley
C) John Tyler
D) James Madison

91. Who was the first President to entertain a ruling monarch?
A) Andrew Johnson
B) Benjamin Harrison
C) Harry Truman
D) Franklin Roosevelt

92. Which President kept a pet mockingbird at the White House?
A) Theodore Roosevelt
B) Richard Nixon
C) Thomas Jefferson
D) James Polk

93. Who was the first governor of a state to become President?
A) John Adams
B) Ronald Reagan
C) Thomas Jefferson
D) Jimmy Carter

94. Which President bathed twice a day in scented bath water, and often stood back away from important visitors to the White House?
A) Millard Fillmore
B) Ulysses S. Grant

C) Dwight Eisenhower
D) William Taft

95. Who said, "I'll be damned if I'm not getting tired of this (the Presidency)."?

96. What President remarked, "When does anyone get any time to think around here?"

97. The Presidential retreat in Maryland was renamed Camp David by Dwight Eisenhower. But for whom was it named?

98. Which First Lady said, following her husband's serious illness, "I am not interested in the President of the United States. I am interested in my husband and his health."?

99. Only two men have reached their 70th birthday in the White House. Ronald Reagan was one of them. Who was the other?

100. Name the President who opened each cabinet meeting with silent prayer.

101. Which Chief Executive had a putting green installed on the south lawn of the White House?

102. More Presidents have belonged to this religious denomination or sect than any other. Name it.

103. Why does the President receive a 21-gun salute?

104. Name the city that was the home and burial site of two Presidents.

105. Who was the first President to draw a salary of $75,000?

106. Which President appointed a 32-year-old man to a high cabinet post?

107. This man was the first President to have a motion picture taken of his inauguration, and was sworn in with a Bible from an African bishop. Name him.

108. Name one of the two Presidents who fought in three separate wars.

109. Which President played the harmonica?

110. Who was the first President to submerge
    in a submarine?

111. Who was the first wife of a President to graduate from college?

112. Who was the only President born in the state of New Jersey?

113. Which President gave up his executive office to the man he took it from?

114. Which President signed a bill establishing 55 miles per hour as the top speed limit on American highways?

115. Who was the first widow of a President to be granted free use of the mail?

116. Which U. S. President had an operation, but kept it secret to prevent the nation from going into a deeper financial depression?

117. Name the President who held a government post at the youngest and the oldest age.

118. Which President, when asked what he wanted for Christmas, replied, "A train set."?

119. Name two of the four Presidents who had sons serve as cabinet members.

120. Who was the first President to attend the launching of a manned space flight?

121. Which President defeated all of the following candidates in his reelection: John Schmitz (American Independent Party), Linda Jenness (Socialist), Louis Fisher (Socialist Labor), Gus Hall (Communist), Earle Munn (Prohibition), John Hospers (Libertarian), Dr. Benjamin Spock (People's Party), John Mahalchik (America First Party), and Gabriel Green (Universal)?

122. Who was the first President to initiate the handshake?

123. Upon this President's death, the United States government made no announcement, completely ignoring his passing. Name him.

124. Presidents John Adams, John Quincy Adams, Millard Fillmore, James Garfield, Chester Arthur, Grover Cleveland, William McKinley, Woodrow Wilson, Warren Harding, Dwight Eisenhower, and Lyndon Johnson all shared something in common regarding their past. What was it?

125. Who was the first President whose mother was alive when he was inaugurated?

126. Which President was the last surviving signer of the Constitution?

127. Name the future President who, upon his twenty-first birthday, received a gift of $1,000,000 from his father.

128. Which man defeated a King to become U.S. President?

129. This man once spent a week exploring and camping at Yellowstone National Park. Later, as President, he took measures to maintain its natural beauty and saved it from commercial exploitation. Name him.

130. Which President defeated the first woman candidate for the Presidency?

131. Name the President who, upon entering the White House, found no books, not even a Bible, and spent some of his own money to create a library.

132. Only one of our Presidents has ever been issued a patent for an invention. Name him.

133. Who was the first successful Presidential candidate to speak German during his campaign?

134. Which President received 85 honorary college degrees, 70 medals, and more than one hundred other honors?

135. Who was the only President to keep the same cabinet for an entire term of office?

136. Which man lived the longest after stepping down as Chief Magistrate?

137. Which man was both the 8th President and the 8th Vice President?

138. Who was the first President to marry while in office?

139. Only one President is buried in New York City. Which one?

140. Who was the first President born in the 19th century?

141. Who was the first President to have impeachment proceedings started against him?

142. Who was the first President to have a veto overridden by Congress?

143. Which President was attacked by piranha fish in Brazil and became stranded in the Amazon Jungle where he asked to be left to die?

144. Which Chief Magistrate was sworn into office by a woman?

145. Four Presidential candidates, all from the same state and all representing the same political party, successfully ran a "front porch campaign." Name two of them.

146. Which man, who wanted only to serve on the U.S. Supreme Court, turned down two requests by the President to serve on the "High Bench"?

The First Ladies Only

147. Which First Lady, while serving earlier as a diplomat's wife, saved Mrs. Lafayette from the guillotine during the French Revolution?

148. Who was the only First Lady born outside the United States?

149. She was the first of the First Ladies to hold a job after marriage. Name her.

150. Harriet Lane was a First Lady and officially served at the White House, though she was never married to a President. Under which President did she serve?

151. Which First Lady stood on her chair to witness the swearing in of her husband as President?

152. This First Lady became the first Presidential wife to ride back to the White House with her husband after inaugural ceremonies. Name her.

153. Can you name the First Lady who died as a result of attending another President's inauguration?

154. Which Chief Executive's wife was called "the first woman to run the government" and nicknamed "The Secret President"?

155. Who was the youngest woman ever to serve as First Lady?

156. This White House hostess banned all alcoholic beverages, card-playing, dancing, and gambling during her husband's term. Name her.

157. Which 19th century First Lady served as the official secretary to the President, a job held only by men in those days?

158. Which First Lady had thousands of Japanese cherry trees planted in the nation's capital?

159. One of our First Ladies has been suspected of poisoning her husband, though no conclusive evidence exists. Who was this?

160. Earlier in her life, this lady was named "Debutante of the Year" in 1947-1948 and later became a newspaper photographer. Name her.

161. Which First Lady opened the East Room to conduct nondenominational Sunday services for hundreds of families?

162. Which First Lady had a daily newspaper column entitled "My Day"?

163. Which First Lady claimed to be a descendant of Pocohontas?

164. According to White House employees and maids, never before or since has a First Lady such as this one owned so many clothes. Name her.

165. Which President referred to his wife as "The Boss"?

166. Which First Lady's actual first name was Thelma?

167. What was the name of President Gerald Ford's pet Siamese cat?

168. The first coast-to-coast paved highway in this country was named after a President. Name him.

169. Who was the first President to veto a Congressional bill?

170. This ex-President attended a college basketball game without paying admission. A 19-year-old student manager

caught up with the former President and asked him to pay the 25¢ admission. He did. Now, can you name either the ex-President or the student manager, who also became President?

171. Only one First Lady of the 20th century gave birth to a child after her 40th birthday. Name her.

172. Which President was a disciple of astrology and studied his horoscope daily?

173. This President hated cats. After he retired from public life, he lived on a farm and ordered that crows or cats seen on his property be shot! Who was this man?

174. Which First Lady once worked as a telephone operator and a movie chorus girl or "hoofer"?

175. What was so unique about the place where Franklin D. Roosevelt wrote his first inaugural address?

176. Which President was presented a 1400-pound block of cheddar cheese, let it ripen or age for two years in the White House, then offered it to the public to celebrate George Washington's birthday?

177. Which President was the son of a shoe salesman and born above a store on Main Street in a small Midwest town?

178. Who was the first President to score a hole-in-one while golfing?

179. Who was the first President to visit all fifty states?

180. Name the President who cancelled all White House tours and placed manned machine guns at the east and west terraces.

181. The Hall of Fame of Great Americans is located at New York University, and nominees are selected every three years. Name the man, also a President, who was the first member of the Hall of Fame.

182. Air Force One, the President's personal airplane, is also known by another name or title. What is it?

183. When General George Armstrong Custer left to fight in the Battle of the Little Big Horn, he departed from a fort in the Dakota Territory. The fort was named after a President. Which one?

184. Name just one of the two Presidents who are buried in Midwest capitals.

185. What was dubbed by the press as "Truman's Folly"?

186. Which President and First Lady had a favorite recipe of peanut soup?

187. This President has been credited with inventing or developing the edible tomato. Name him.

188. Which First Lady served as the official hostess at all state functions *before* her husband became President?

189. Harry Truman kept two mottoes on his desk. One small sign stated, "The Buck Stops Here." What did the other sign read?

190. Which President was so unpopular that an influenza epidemic at the time was named after him?

191. Which President was also Speaker of the House at one time?

192. During his race for the Presidency, this candidate's campaign manager remarked that this future President had a "weirdo factor." Name the successful candidate.

193. Which President said, "This administration will be cussed and discussed for many years to come."?

194. This 19th century President planted a magnolia tree on the South Portico lawn. Name him.

195. Technically, one of our Presidents is not buried in any state. Can you name him?

196. Two Presidents have graduated from Yale. Name one.

197. Which President is buried near the Professional Football Hall of Fame?

198. Which President was usually late to his own meetings and carried a basket filled with official-looking documents to give the impression he had been working?

199. Which state has ten mountain peaks named in honor of our Presidents?

200. Which President often went "skinny dipping in the Potomac and once had his clothes stolen, leaving him "in the buff"?

Hidden Word Puzzle

See page 161 for answers.

Hidden in each sentence below is the name of one of our Presidents. Find the President's last name and either circle or underline it. Good hunting!

1. We will arrive in Phoenix on the fifth of April.

2. Policeman Mike Forshay estimated the thieves took forty dollars.

3. Won't you please stay, Lora, and help us with our chores?

4. A hard ingratitude shows very little politeness.

5. Mary and Judy once saw Senator Fred Harris on the train.

6. General Douglas MacArthur was awarded the Congressional Medal of Honor.

7. Thousands of immigrants helped to build Ohio's network of canals.

8. The corner tavern is without rum and whiskey to sell.

9. The Indians, Browns and Cavaliers are all teams in Cleveland.

10. Who over there has the *Akron Beacon Journal* to read?

11. Don had to stay after school for detention because he was chewing gum.

12. When I was nine years old, my sisters didn't let me play jacks on the floor.

13. You cannot go out at night after ten o'clock because of the curfew.

14. While working in the sugar fields, one has to be careful of snakes.

15. Along with her French husband, Madam Serain flew to London.

16. Sue has taken Ned yellow roses since he has been in the hospital.

17. Ralph has lots of money and wants to buy a car terribly.

18. To build airstrips in Korea, gangs of unskilled laborers were used.

19. Rose hasn't been to a happier ceremony since her wedding last March.

20. The Mills Brothers once sang at John's One-Way Nightclub.

Matching

All answers begin on page 161.

Many of our Chief Magistrates have had more than one nickname, or a nickname not widely known except during their own time. Match the following monikers with the respective Presidents.

1. Great White Chief	A. George Washington
2. Napoleon of the Stump	B. Andrew Jackson
3. Turncoat or Honest	C. Theodore Roosevelt
4. Wobbly Willie	D. Chester Arthur
5. Tycoon or Great Emancipator	E. Woodrow Wilson
6. Atlas of America	F. Benjamin Harrison
7. Dude President	G. Lyndon Johnson
8. Light Bulb	H. James Polk
9. Scribe of the Revolution	I. John Tyler
10. Chinese	J. William McKinley
11. Phrasemaker	K. Abraham Lincoln
12. Pointed Arrow or Sharp Knife	L. Thomas Jefferson

Susan B. Anthony is the only non-President to appear on contemporary coins. Match the following coins with the proper Presidential portrait.

1. penny	A. Franklin D. Roosevelt
2. quarter	B. Thomas Jefferson
3. half dollar	C. George Washington
4. dime	D. John Kennedy
5. nickel	E. Abraham Lincoln
6. dollar	F. Dwight Eisenhower

Match the following Presidents with their favorite horses.

1. The General	A. Zachary Taylor
2. Whitey and Claybank	B. Abraham Lincoln
3. Old Bob	C. Ulysses S. Grant
4. Egypt and Cincinnatus	D. John Tyler
5. Texas	E. Theodore Roosevelt

Few Presidents have served their country without having some scandal, either preceding or during their adminstration. Match the scandals with the respective Presidents.

1. Star Routes Frand and Whiskey Ring	A. Harding
2. Teapot Dome and Veterans Bureau	B. Truman
3. Crédit Mobilier	C. Grant
4. Watergate and Milk Fund	D. Garfield
5. Peggy Eaton Affair	E. Jackson
6. Veterans Administration	F. Nixon

More nicknames. Match these men with their nicknames.

1. Gentleman Boss	A. John Quincy Adams
2. The Mad Messiah	B. Chester Alan Arthur
3. Kid Gloves	C. Ulysses S. Grant
4. Old Man Eloquent	D. Benjamin Harrison
5. The Galena Tanner	E. Theodore Roosevelt

Listed below are some quotes attributed to our Presidents. But be careful! Some of these quotations may surprise you; they were said by Presidents at a time before, during or after their

53

terms in office. Some of these quotes later came back to haunt these men.

1. "I shall say it again and again and again—your boys are not going to be sent into any foreign wars."

2. "Jews make the best Republicans."

3. "Any people anywhere, being inclined and having the power, have the right to rise up and shake off the existing government, and form a new one that suits them better."

4. "The Union—it must be preserved!"

5. "I am not a crook."

6. "We have room for but one language here, and that is the English language, for we intend to see that the crucible turns our people out as Americans."

7. "No man will labor for himself who can make another labor for him."

8. "I have had all of Washington that I want; I never had the complex of being a big shot."

Choices

A. Abraham Lincoln	E. William H. Taft
B. Franklin D. Roosevelt	F. Harry Truman
C. Richard Nixon	G. Thomas Jefferson
D. Andrew Jackson	H. Theodore Roosevelt

Match the respective Presidents with their pet dogs.

1. Laddie Boy—airedale	A. Gerald Ford
2. Murray of Falahill (Fala)—Scottie	B. Woodrow Wilson
3. Wolf—wolfhound	C. Calvin Coolidge
4. Fido—small yellow mixed breed	D. John Kennedy
5. Heidi—weimaraner	E. Warren Harding
6. Liberty—golden retriever	F. Dwight Eisenhower
7. Rob Roy—collie	G. Lyndon Johnson
8. Him and Her—beagles	H. Franklin D. Roosevelt
9. Davie—airedale	I. Abraham Lincoln
10. Drunkard and Sweet Lips—hounds	J. George Washington

Match the Presidential yachts with the respective Chief Executives.

1. Sequoia	A. Truman
2. Benedict	B. T. Roosevelt, Taft, Coolidge, Wilson,
3. Honey Fitz	and Harding
4. Williamsburg	C. Cleveland
5. Mayflower	D. F. D. Roosevelt and Nixon
	E. Kennedy

Match the Presidential signatures below with the following clues for that President.

1. Father of our country

2. President for just one month

3. Served in office during the Mexican War

4. Victor at Shiloh and Vicksburg

5. President for two non-consecutive terms

6. Former Ohio newspaper man

7. Defeated Nixon in a narrow vote

8. Scientist, inventor and musician

9. Also a Senate Majority Leader

A. *James K. Polk*

B. *Grover Cleveland*

C. *Warren G. Harding*

D. *John F. Kennedy*

E. *W H Harrison*

F. *Andrew Jackson*

G. *U. S. Grant*

H. *G Washington*

I. *Th Jefferson*

It Happened Like This...

Lincoln Got His Goat

Abe Lincoln made frequent visits to the Soldiers Home each summer. Once he piled Tad and two pet goats into a carriage. A shocked Presidential aide tactfully suggested that the goats shouldn't ride in the carriage. Lincoln responded, "Why not? There's plenty of room in here." The goats went. The aide stayed.

On Second Thought...

When John Adams was in school, he begged his father to allow him to quit studying Latin, a subject he found boring and difficult. After numerous pleas, the elderly Adams granted his son's request, and suggested he try ditch-digging. For two days the future President dug ditches on the farm. Exhausted and humiliated, John had a change of priorities, remarking, "Toil conquered pride." Soon thereafter, he returned to studying Latin to prepare for college.

To The Point

James K. Polk was a man of little humor and no nonsense. John Quincy Adams once used these adjectives to describe the eleventh President: "has not wit, no literature, no point of argument, no philosophy..."

Sorry We Mentioned It

A group of temperance women and prohibitionists urged President Chester Arthur to stop drinking, and also to cease serving alcoholic beverages in the White House. His reply left no doubts in the minds of his visitors. "Ladies," he said, "I may be President of the United States, but my private life is nobody's damn business!"

A Warning from the Old Warrior

During his campaign for the Presidency in 1840, William Henry Harrison told a group of Ohio citizens, "See to the government. See that the government does not acquire too much power. Keep a check upon your rulers. Do this, and liberty is safe."

Family Fame

Abe Lincoln was related to Paul Revere. Lincoln's father, Thomas, was the cousin of Amos and Jedediah Lincoln, both of whom were sons-in-law of the famous silversmith.

What Game Was That?

John Tyler was supposedly on his knees playing marbles with his children when he learned William Henry Harrison had died. Other sources, however, state Tyler was playing horseshoes with two sons in the yard of his Virginia home. Take your pick.

Whoa There!

President Benjamin Harrison's grandson had a pet billy goat that pulled the boy in a wagon. One day the goat ran away with the boy, and the President had to dash down Pennsylvania Avenue to rescue his grandson.

Now You Know

Harriet Lane, the niece of President James Buchanan, served as the official White House hostess. She was without doubt one of the most popular First Ladies of the nineteenth century.

Her stunning good looks and charm made her the envy of many Americans. A Navy vessel, commissioned in 1857, was named in her honor. The popular song "Listen to the Mockingbird" was dedicated to her. In addition, streets, towns, clubs and hairdos were named after her. Wrote one observer, "Not since Abigail Adams had the President's home seen so brilliant a life. Harriet was the perfect hostess, with a gift for tact and diplomacy rarely seen."

I Gotta Stay

In 1849, Abraham Lincoln served on a committee for President Zachary Taylor's inaugural ball. The party was a great success, but Lincoln stayed very late. He couldn't find his hat.

Tippecanoe's Downfall

During his inaugural ceremonies, William Henry Harrison fainted twice, and was revived by friends who rubbed whisky on his temples. Though exhausted, the President insisted on attending all of the ceremonies. Earlier in the day he gave a long inaugural speech in bitter cold, but did so without a hat or overcoat. In trying to demonstrate his frontier toughness, Harrison fell ill and died just one month later. Some feel his age of 68 years contributed to this.

Big Spender

While serving as First Lady, Mary Todd Lincoln once purchased more than 300 pairs of expensive gloves in a four-month period. One bolt of lace she owned was valued at $4,000. One of her shawls cost $2,000, a parasol at $250, and one handkerchief cost $80. Her expensive tastes often troubled the President. In 1875, her son, Robert, had her committed to an insane asylum near Chicago. She was later released and died in 1882.

How's That?

Booth saved Lincoln's life! That's right. One day while Robert Lincoln was waiting for a train, he slipped off the station platform into the path of an oncoming train. Suddenly he was jerked up by his coat collar and rescued just in time. His rescuer was the famous actor, Edwin Booth, brother of the future assassin.

"The Baby"

For three months Lyndon Johnson had no first or middle name. Before mom and dad finally agreed on the name, the future President was simply called "the baby." His first name was chosen in honor of a family friend, W. C. Linden.

We Told You So

It was said of Lincoln's first Secretary of War, Simon Cameron, that he would steal everything except a "red hot stove." Perhaps, as a warning, Lincoln mentioned this phrase to Cameron, who is credited with responding, "An honest politician is one who, when he is bought, will stay bought." In a matter of weeks the War Department was in disarray and Cameron was dismissed, replaced by the fiercely independent Edwin Stanton.

Changing Hands

In a five-week period, our country had three different Presidents. This was in 1841 when Martin Van Buren, William Henry Harrison and John Tyler served in office. Harrison died just four weeks after succeeding Van Buren.

Darn....Those Slippers!

Though First Lady Ida McKinley did not attend many White House functions due to her ill health, she kept very busy. She knitted more than 3500 pairs of slippers. Most of these were donated to charities, while some were sold at fairs or auctioned off at benefits, bringing in large amounts of money for the needy.

A Strange Looking Plant, Indeed

George Washington grew marijuana. The wealthy Virginia farmer imported seeds from all over the world and planted hundreds of crops at Mt. Vernon. He was trying to grow hemp for cloth and rope. Incidentally, Teddy Roosevelt and Lyndon Johnson ordered it grown by the government for research and medical purposes.

Sneaking In Some Snoozes

Presidents Taft and Coolidge both were notorious nap-takers. Coolidge got plenty of sleep, sometimes as much as eleven hours a day. Taft, on the other hand, often embarrassed those around him by slumbering off. He fell asleep at Cabinet meetings, White House dinners, church sermons and funerals. Once, he even "dozed off" in an open car during a campaign tour in New York City!

Aw, Nuts!

President Eisenhower didn't like squirrels. It seems they dug up holes on his golfing green and hid nuts in them. Sometimes "Ike" would putt a golfball right at the cup, only to have it roll by due to a squirrel's landscaping job. The President would shake his club and yell, "Get those goddam squirrels out of here!"

Pay Up!

James A. Garfield's funeral was never paid for. Mr. Speare, the undertaker, repeatedly submitted a bill for $1890.50 to the United States government, but never received one penny.

Losers

Many Presidents suffered setbacks in their political career before entering the White House. James Polk was defeated twice for the governorship of Tennessee. James Buchanan twice lost the Democratic nomination for President. Benjamin Harrison lost a bid for the U. S. Senate and governor of Indiana. Teddy Roosevelt lost a race for mayor of New York. Richard Nixon lost in elections for the Presidency and governor of California.

Where Is He?

During his second term, Woodrow Wilson stayed out of the Presidential office for a seventeen-month period. His absence was due to a stroke he suffered in October of 1919. His wife tried her best to keep his condition a secret and even Wilson's closest aides and friends were not permitted to see him. He was nursed back to health, but not before Mrs. Wilson had made numerous political decisions.

An Eye For An Eye

President John Adams sent a special message to Congress when his son and future President, John Quincy, was slapped in the face by Russel Jarvis at the Capitol. Jarvis was the editor of a Washington, D.C. newspaper, and when the President requested a congressional investigation, no official report was ever filed.

Pass Me By

Mrs. Theodore Roosevelt did not like to shake hands. To avoid this gesture she held a large bouquet of flowers with both hands and politely bowed to each guest in the receiving line. Her husband, quite the contrary, was a notorious handshaker.

Don't Worry Mom

Perhaps no child ran away more often than Lyndon Johnson. From the time he could walk, the independent child wandered far off from his rural Texas home. His expeditions were so frequent that his parents gave up paddling him. On one occasion, he hid in a haystack near the house while his frantic and frustrated mother sat down and cried right beside it. Young Lyndon enjoyed listening to his mother sob, and stayed in the haystack for a couple more hours.

Short Term Economics

Andrew Jackson was the only President to pay off the national debt. He withdrew government funds from the national bank, but this move had a bad effect on his successor's Presidency. In 1837, the country experienced a severe financial panic and Martin Van Buren "took the heat."

A Chip Off the Old Block

Like father, like son—sometimes. One of President John Adams' last official acts was removing his son, John Quincy, from his ambassadorship to Prussia (now Germany). In so doing, Adams deprived his successor, Thomas Jefferson, the satisfaction of dismissing him. The second and third Presidents were political opponents, but when the younger Adams returned home, he was elected to the U. S. Senate and became a strong supporter of Jefferson. Bostonians regarded this as an act of treason and never forgave the future President for switching parties and taking sides with a man who was a devout enemy of the "upper crust" of society. The "Blue Bloods" of Boston should have realized that such a trait of independence was often demonstrated by members of the Adams family.

How Low Can You Go?

Prior to the Civil War, Ulysses Grant was desperately poor. After several failures in the business world, he went to St. Louis where for a time he collected trash, reselling it for a small income. In 1858, he even pawned his watch to buy Christmas gifts for his family. But the advent of the Great Rebellion gave Grant, and men like him, an opportunity to demonstrate their latent talents of courage, determination and leadership.

A Mass of Misnomers

Presidents Grant and Cleveland had many nicknames. Grant was referred to as "The Butcher," "American Caesar," "Old Three Stars," "Great Hammerer," "Uncle Sam," "United States," "Unconditional Surrender," and "Useless Sole." Cleveland was called, "Old Veto," "The Buffalo Hangman," "Sage of Princeton," "Stuffed Prophet," and "Uncle Jumbo."

The Missing Prepositions

Following Lee's surrender in April of 1865, President Lincoln spoke to a crowd outside the White House. The joyous throng was anxious to hear some words from their victorious President. Many of the people gathered there were well aware of Lincoln's plans of mercy and generosity towards the rebel states, but the mood of this particular audience seemed to want revenge and punishment. Young Tad Lincoln listened to his father's conciliatory remarks, and then heard Senator Harlan pose the question loudly, "What shall we do with the rebels?" When the crowd shouted, "Hang 'em, hang 'em," Tad turned to his father saying, "No, no papa. Not hang them. Hang *on to* them." Lincoln, with a twinkle in his eye, happily cried out, "That's it—Tad has got it. We must hang *on to* them."

Flame Brains

We've had several red-heads as President. James Garfield, Thomas Jefferson, Martin Van Buren and John Kennedy were all "carrot tops."

Within the Wife's Earshot

Entertainer Vicki Carr once sang at a White House reception held by Gerald Ford. After meeting the President, she asked Ford, "What's your favorite dish?" Replied the President, "You are." Having heard this comment, First Lady Betty Ford stated, "*That* woman will never get into the White House again." A few days later Mrs. Ford walked into the west wing and found a large photo of Vicki Carr in a beguiling dress hanging there. She simply laughed and turned the picture to the wall.

Schoolhouse Rebel

At the age of eleven, John Tyler was the ringleader in a rebellion against one of his teachers. A tyrannical schoolmaster, one Mr. McMurdo, enjoyed using the birch rod on his pupils for even the slightest provocations. Young John conspired with a group of boys to lead a revolt, and one day at school McMurdo was tackled and shackled. With hands and feet bound, he was left inside the building. After a couple of hours crying out for help, McMurdo was freed when a passerby heard his screams. Tyler's father defended his son's actions.

Advice Not Taken

In 1887, President Grover Cleveland was introduced to a five-year-old boy and his parents at the White House. Cleveland looked down at the youth and said, "My little man, I am making a strange wish for you. It is that you may never be President of the United States." But the boy didn't listen, because in 1933, he took the oath of office as our 32nd President— Franklin Delano Roosevelt.

Flying Muck

President Truman did not like Ohio—that is to say he did not like the home state of Senator Robert A. Taft, a political opponent who was nicknamed "Mr. Republican." It is a true story that when Truman flew home to Missouri in the Presidential plane, Independence, he made certain the pilot flew over the "Buckeye State." Why? It seems that's when he used the toilet on board the airplane, and as Truman flew over the friendly skies of Ohio, he ordered the "Presidential payload" dumped. I guess this was his way of saying, "Take that, Taft!"

Two of Yours for "Babe"

President Hoover was once asked to autograph a piece of paper *twice* by a boy. When the President asked why the youth wanted two signatures, he was told, "You see, it takes two of yours in trade to get one of Babe Ruth's." The wish was granted.

Don't Apologize

During the War Between the States, President Lincoln went to see Secretary of War Edwin Stanton. Upon entering the War Department building he was nearly knocked down by an on-rushing Union officer, apparently in a great hurry. Upon recognizing his Commander-in-Chief, the officer offered "10,000 pardons." Lincoln simply smiled and said, "Once is enough. I wish the whole army would charge like that."

Now That's Service!

Dolley Madison was one of our most beautiful and gracious First Ladies. She entertained lavishly, selecting her guests with great care for the sake of hospitality and congeniality. At most White House dinners she hired Negro waiters for 35¢ an evening, and assigned one to each guest at the dinner table.

Whiter Than White

President George Washington owned a beautiful white stallion, and always had his grooms apply a coat of white paint to the animal before making a public appearance. When the paint dried, the horse was brushed and buffed. Even the hooves were manicured and touched up with black paint to intensify the gleaming contrast.

I Hear You Knockin', But You Can't Come In

Things often got crowded for the Benjamin Harrison family. At one time, eleven members of his family lived at the White House, sharing just one bathroom among themselves. Perhaps that's one reason the twenty-third President didn't mind being defeated in the next election.

It Could Have "Bugs"

Pushinka, a small white-haired dog, was the daughter of the Russian space dog Strelka. It was presented as a gift to the Kennedys by the Russian leader, Nikita Krushchev. The Secret Service made certain the pet was not "bugged" internally as a "spy dog." Pushinka became a favorite with the Kennedy children, performing tricks and entertaining friends. When puppies were born, JFK referred to them as "pupniks."

Oh, Just One More Thing...

During an interview with a noted newspaperman, Calvin Coolidge answered each question with "no comment." As the frustrated reporter was leaving, the President shouted, "By the way, don't quote me."

Come Back Here!

Andrew Johnson was a runaway slave. As an indentured servant, Johnson escaped, and his owner put advertisements in the newspapers to get him back.

Just a Little Bit Closer

Jimmy Carter was the first President who insisted on having the Vice President with an office located in the White House. Walter "Fritz" Mondale had his headquarters in the west wing, and Carter conferred with him regularly.

Hot Times at the White House

The Executive Mansion has been damaged several times by fire. The most extensive damage was when the British set it aflame in

1814, completely destroying the interior. A small blaze occurred during Van Buren's term, and another fire, on December 24, 1929, destroyed part of the west wing.

To Jimmy's Surprise

While visiting with Egypt's President Anwar Sadat, Jimmy Carter was given a tour of the Great Pyramid of Giza. The guide explained to the American President that it took twenty years to build. Remarked Carter, "I'm surprised that a government organization could do it that quickly."

Whippin' em into Shape

Teaching in a one-room log schoolhouse was no easy task. In the fall of 1849, seventeen-year-old Jim Garfield was asked to replace a schoolmaster in Solon, Ohio. Offered $48.00 for a four-month term, he decided to take the job. Though inexperienced, he was one of the few teachers who could solve long division. But there was a problem. Some ruffians had driven away the last two teachers, and two of the ringleaders were older and bigger than Garfield. On his first day in class he was put to the test. The rookie instructor asked the pupils to please rise for a recitation. "But we don't feel like standin', teacher," came the reply from one good-size, indignant youth. Then, in the next moment, Garfield was hit in the head with a block of wood. Calmly, the teacher put his book down and walked over to his assailant. Suddenly, arms and legs entangled in wild confusion. The other pupils scattered as the two young men "gave it a go." When the fighting stopped, Garfield's tormentor lay dazed on the floor. Opening the door, he grabbed the defeated dunce and tossed him out by the seat of his pants. Class continued uninterrupted, and the next day Garfield entered the school with a bullwhip. "I'll use this if I have to," he announced. But his point had been made, and there was never any need for it.

Who Am I?

At one of President Cleveland's receptions, a man named Decker stood in line waiting to meet the Chief Executive. Mr. Decker gave his name to Colonel Williams, the President's aide, remarking that his name was easy to pronounce and remember. The Colonel presented him to Cleveland. While shaking his hand, Cleveland said, "Happy to meet you, Mr. Cracker." First Lady Francis Cleveland beamed, "Happy to meet you, Mr. Baker." Miss Bayard, also in the reception line, said, "Mr. Sacker." And Mrs. Whitney exclaimed, "Happy to meet you, Mr. Black." As Mr. Decker left, he looked at his calling card to make certain what his name was.

Getting to the Point

During his second term Richard Nixon grew increasingly nervous and frustrated, no doubt due in part to the Watergate scandal. On one occasion, in trying to sign a congressional bill before several representatives and the press, he put the cover *on* the pen. Then, realizing his error, he removed the cover but dropped the pen and cover on the floor. An embarrassed President finally got it figured out.

Valuable Companions

Sarah Polk and Bess Truman worked hand-in-hand with their husbands in drafting speeches, issuing press releases and making political decisions. They played an important role in their spouse's administration. In addition, Abigail Adams assisted her husband, John, on political matters.

He Calmed the Angry Sea

In July of 1883, Andrew Jackson went for a ride down the Chesapeake on an old steamboat. The weather took a turn for the worse as waves began to rock the boat. A worried guest expressed fear for the safety of the passengers and crew. Jackson looked at the elderly gentleman and said, ''You are uneasy—you never sailed with *me* before, I see." In a short time the tempest passed and all arrived safely. Such incidents added to the belief that Jackson was guided and protected by Divine Providence.

Haunted Mansion

President William Henry Harrison's ghost has been reported probing around in the White House attic, so believed several White House personnel during the first half of the twentieth century. During Truman's administration the Executive Mansion underwent complete renovation and stories of "Old Tippecanoe's Ghost" ceased. In addition, reports of Lincoln's ghost and that of Abigail Adams have been published in past years.

Who's He?

At one time John Hanson was regarded as a U. S. President. Prior to George Washington's first term, the Maryland political leader was chosen as President of the U. S. Congress in 1781.

Dry Up!

After visiting Venice on a world tour, ex-President Grant suggested the city, where canals served as streets, would look much better drained.

A Multi-Talented Man

Thomas Jefferson and Theodore Roosevelt were men with diverse interests. But few have had a more varied background than James Garfield. A true success story, this man rose from humble beginnings to hold the most powerful position in the land. He was, at one time or another, a farmer, sailor, custodian, teacher, Civil War General, minister, college president, lawyer, legislator and philosopher. As a Congressman for seventeen years in Washington, the Ohio-bred lawmaker liked to "show off" his amazing ability of writing with both hands at the same time. He would ask a visitor to come into his office and recite a poem in English. Then, he proceeded to interpret the poem and write it out on two pieces of paper, writing the interpretation in Greek and another in Latin.

Is There Another Bid?

A few years ago, a laundry bill signed by George Washington was sold at an auction for $1100. Dated 1787, it was signed by Washington and two fellow officers. Signatures of the first President command high prices, some exceeding $12,000 for signed and dated documents.

Shades of Sorrow

First Lady Jane Pierce was often referred to as "The Shadow of the White House." Attractive, deeply religious and frail, Mrs. Pierce lost three sons prior to her husband's rise to the Presidency. Their last son, Benny, died in a train wreck while Pierce was President-elect. She wore black for the rest of her life and hardly ever appeared in public. Supposedly, she blamed her husband's involvement in politics as the cause for much of their grief. Frank Pierce went to Washington in 1853 as a broken man. It was a time period in our history which called for strong leadership; Civil War loomed ahead, but the country would have to wait eight more years when an Illinois lawyer took a strong stand on the issues of secession and slavery.

Smoke-filled Room

According to tradition, President Taylor's wife, Margaret (also called Peggy), smoked a corn cob pipe in the privacy of her room at the White House. Though she appeared in public and entertained guests in her upstairs sitting room, Margaret Taylor never took part in formal social functions.

Come On In, Fellas

In the true spirit of democracy, President Tom Jefferson invited his butcher to a formal White House dinner. The butcher, however, brought along his uninvited son. Jefferson happily received them both and saw to it they were well fed.

Wishful Thinking

During his recovery in the hospital from an assassin's near-fatal bullet, President Ronald Reagan exclaimed, "If I had this much attention in Hollywood, I'd have stayed there!"

Another Tribute For "Silent Cal"

Upon hearing the news of Calvin Coolidge's death in January of 1933, Clarence Darrow, the famed trial lawyer, said Coolidge "was the greatest man who ever came out of Plymouth Corner, Vermont."

I'm Sorry—It Was Just a Joke

On more than one occasion, Lincoln's wisecracks got him into trouble. In 1842, he made some critical remarks about another Illinois politician, James Shields. Challenged to a duel, Lincoln was asked his choice of weapons. "How about cow dung at five paces?", suggested the prairie lawyer. But Shields was not in good humor and insisted that Lincoln and he use swords. Just before the duel took place, Lincoln apologized and the contest was cancelled.

No Thanks

Arthur Krock, noted journalist and author for many years, tells of a story involving his grandfather's second son. Grandpa took the seventeen-year-old boy to the White House to meet President Rutherford B. Hayes. When the youth was introduced to the President, he put his hands behind his back and remarked, "I decline to shake hands with the man who stole the election from Tilden."

That's Telling Them

FDR was elected four times to the Presidency. To prevent this happening ever again, Congress passed a resolution limiting the term of office to just two terms. When asked to comment on the law, incumbent Harry Truman said, "When they passed that limitation on the Presidency, Congress should have had enough guts and honesty to limit their own tenure, too."

Finding a Needle in a Haystack

Like many of our earlier Presidents, Abraham Lincoln was constantly besieged by job hunters and office seekers. One man in particular impressed him, and after an interview Lincoln gave him a note which read, "This man wants to work—so uncommon a want that I think it ought to be gratified."

Boys will be "Boys"

Abe Lincoln pulled his share of pranks as a youngster. Convincing some of his friends to wade into a mud puddle, he picked them up and carried them one by one into his stepmother's house. There they proceeded to track their muddy feet across the ceiling. To accomplish this special effect, Lincoln held each one *upside down*.

Written in the Stars

Andrew Johnson, our seventeenth President, was born under the sign of Capricorn. His horoscope reads: "Ambitious, reserved and rigid. Extreme likes and dislikes. Conservative. Not easily swayed. A fighter and a hard worker." Nixon was also a Capricorn. Seems to fit, doesn't it?

Honest Jim

James Buchanan, our fifteenth President, served his country well. He had a long record of public service both in the United States and abroad. Though he was considered a weak, ineffectual leader, he was a man of high integrity. Buchanan made it a rule never to accept gifts of any kind from friends or supporters.

"Puddling" the Newspaper

John Kennedy had a feud with the *New York Herald-Tribune* and banned the paper from the White House. Traphes Bryant, the kennel keeper, got a copy of the newspaper, cut it up, and lined a puppy box with it. Knowing the President would inspect the puppies, Bryant arranged it so the newspaper's name hung over the top of the box. Kennedy spotted it right away, smiled and nodded approvingly. Turning to Bryant he beamed, "It's finally found its proper use."

Home Improvements

Did one of our First Ladies invent air conditioning? You be the judge. When James Garfield was shot in early July of 1881, he was taken back to the White House to recover. The heat and humidity in the nation's capital was almost unbearable. To comfort her ailing husband, Lucretia Garfield called upon the Navy Department to cool down the room where the mortally-wounded President lay. With a series of fans, wetted sheets, air ducts and a charcoal filtering system which she helped design, the temperature of the room was considerably lowered. Unfortunately, Garfield suffered great pain as probing doctors failed to locate the bullet. Losing a hundred pounds during a twelve-week period, Garfield lost his fight for survival at a New Jersey resort in September. Perhaps, at her husband's expense, "Crete" Garfield made a valuable contribution to science.

Just Take the Basket

In February of 1865, President Lincoln, Secretary of State Seward and three other government officials met with representatives of the Confederacy to discuss settling the Civil War. The two parties met on board a Union transport ship near Hampton Roads, Va. Following lengthy, but fruitless discussions concerning freed slaves and the readmission of states, the two sides shook hands and cordially parted. The Confederate commissioners were put in a rowboat and taken back to their steamer. Just before leaving, they noticed heading towards them a rowboat with a former black slave at the oars. Upon reaching the deck he presented the southerners with a basket of champagne and a note with compliments from Seward and Lincoln. Yelling through a megaphone aboard the Union ship, the words of Seward were clear to the departing rebels, "Keep the champagne, but return the Negro."

Is This O.K.?

The popular expression, "O.K." has its origin with two different Presidential candidates. It was used when Democrat Martin Van Buren, nicknamed "Old Kinderhook," ran for President in 1836 against the Whig nominee, William Henry Harrison. The initials of this epithet became a password meaning "all is right." Van Buren won. Later, in the Presidential campaign of 1840, Harrison (again nominated by the Whigs) was speaking at a rally in Urbana, Ohio, where a large sign on a wagon bore a crude but well-meant slogan: "The people is Oll Korect." Another Harrison supporter, an innkeeper on the National Road near Springfield, Ohio, named his place the "OK Tavern." Democratic opponents criticized the bad spelling and pointed to the ignorance of Harrison's supporters, but the effort backfired. Harrison won. His opponent, incidentally, was the incumbent President, Martin Van Buren!

Burning Proof

With Theodore Roosevelt as a witness, former cabinet member Robert Lincoln burned some papers in a fireplace. When asked what documents he was destroying, Robert Lincoln replied, "It would serve no purpose to make them public. They deal with a man who played a part in my father's death—a man of my father's cabinet." Historians familiar with the Lincoln conspiracy believe Secretary of War Edwin Stanton, or Secretary of the Treasury Salmon P. Chase, could have been the man whose identity Robert Lincoln was concealing.

Save That Floor!

James Garfield was shot in the back by Charles Guiteau on July 2, 1881, in the Baltimore and Potomac Railroad Depot (long since torn down). The carpeted floor, stained with Garfield's blood, was preserved and sent to the Smithsonian Institution nearby.

Not a Draft Dodger!

Grover Cleveland was drafted into the Union Army in 1863, but he didn't go. Instead he paid for a substitute to take his place. This was a common practice in those days. Cleveland's two older brothers were already in uniform, and they felt he should stay home and take care of their widowed mother.

A Matter of Interpretation

It was during the Mexican War when the 30th Congress was in session. Representatives from the state of Illinois, including the young Whig congressman by the name of Abe Lincoln, got into a brief discussion on how to pronounce the name of their state. Some insisted it was "Ill-e-noy," while others said it was "Illanoise." One of the members appealed to John Quincy Adams who voiced, "If one were to judge from the character of the representatives in the Congress from that state, I should decide unhesitatingly that the proper pronunciation was 'All noise'!"

I Shouldn't Have Said That

All Presidents have suffered from lipus linguis—or slips of the tongue. Because of the mass media and all the attention they get, today's Chief Executives receive undue criticism when they make an errant remark. Gerald Ford certainly had his share, once addressing the students at Iowa State as "Ohio State." In Pinehurst, North Carolina, he attended the World Golf Hall of Fame Classic and remarked into a microphone, "I sit in front of the television and take a pile of work, and in between this shot and that shot, I try to concentrate."

Finding a Loophole

When Lincoln issued the Emancipation Proclamation to free the slaves, he signed it as Commander-in-Chief. Thus, he technically avoided breaking the law of the Constitution which permitted the existence of slavery (the law was also upheld by the U. S. Supreme Court in 1857). Lincoln's document went into effect on January 1, 1863 as a military measure. Sneaky!

Forgotten Leader

James K. Polk was one of our most able leaders, and during his term, our nation made some great strides. Polk had a lot of enemies because of his stand on slavery and other issues, including a controversial war with Mexico. During his campaign, Polk made only three or four promises and kept them all. While in the White House, the country experienced many changes: the U. S. Naval Academy at Annapolis was established; Wisconsin, Iowa and Texas were added to the Union; the sewing machine was invented; gold was discovered in California; postage stamps were first used to send letters; the U. S. acquired much territory by defeating Santa Anna and the Mexicans; the Smithsonian Institution was founded; the rotary press was invented and revolutionized the printing industry; the Mormons settled in Utah; Cyrus McCormick began production of the reaper; Morse invented the telegraph; a Women's Rights Convention was held; Associated Press was established; and Longfellow, Emerson, Lowell and Melville became recognized men of letters. Historians often cite these advances, but fail to mention James Polk in conjunction with them.

Having Their Say Too

Coolidge was criticized once by Herbert Hoover for appointing a certain millionaire-industrialist to the Cabinet. A friend of Hoover's also complained, telling Coolidge, "Mr. President, that fellow is a son of a bitch." "Well," said Coolidge, "don't you think *they* ought to be represented too?"

Lower Your Cameras, Boys

In some ways, Lyndon Johnson was very particular about having his picture taken. Photographers were informed the President wished to be photographed from the left side. On the other hand, Johnson didn't hesitate in showing his gall-bladder surgical scar on his belly to the press.

This is Ridiculous

Servants and employees at the White House often found it difficult working for Richard Nixon, though they never admitted it publicly at the time. New rules and regulations, firing and hiring personnel, and constant "nit-picking" by the President and his staff created an atmosphere of sobriety and suspicion. One of Nixon's quirks was building a fire in the Lincoln sitting room in July. Running the air conditioning at top capacity, Nixon lowered the room temperature to below 50 degrees so he could sit before the fireplace. Even Nixon aides, including Bob Haldeman, were seen carrying logs, stoking the fire and hauling ashes in midsummer when temperatures approached 100 degrees outside.

Flattery May Get You Somewhere

It was James Madison, our fourth President, who said, "A little flattery will support a man through great fatigue."

They Can Thank Mom

Ex-President Nixon was asked if possibly one of his daughters might someday become President. It was his opinion that we will see a woman as Chief Executive. Commenting further, he said, "Both Julie and Tricia are very intelligent. Of course I would say that because they take after their mother."

The Big Roundup

Chester Arthur was a quartermaster in the Union Army stationed in New York City. Following the Union defeat at Bull Run, several companies of northern Zouaves returned to the city. Roaming at will, they presented a threat to the citizenry. Theft, vagrancies and loitering posted a heavy burden on the New York Police Department. Young Mr. Arthur used his authority and had 400 of these soldiers arrested, confined on board a ship, and sent back to the army where they were consolidated into a new regiment.

Overindulgence

A President who died from eating too much ice cream? Yes, it did happen, at least indirectly. When Zachary Taylor collapsed at the afternoon July 4th ceremonies, at the time held at the site of the Washington Monument, he was hurried back to the White House. It was extremely warm that summer day in 1850, and to cool off, he ordered large amounts of cold drinks and frozen desserts. That same evening he suffered severe indigestion, caught cold, developed pneumonia, and died days later.

A Shocking Experience

Benjamin Harrison was the first President to have electric lights in the White House. However, he was afraid to turn them on for fear of being shocked. He even refused to push electric bells and buzzers.

Following in Dad's Footsteps

Caroline Harrison, daughter of our twenty-third President, Benjamin Harrison, became the first President of the National Daughters of the Revolution, better known as the D.A.R.

Hands Off

Washington's estate, Mt. Vernon, was never inhabited by Union or Confederate forces during the Civil War. Both sides agreed that it was neutral ground, and no armed soldiers ever invaded the home. That would have made George very happy.

"Time Out," Mr. Lincoln!

In 1860, the Republican National Convention met in Chicago. When the delegates finally decided on their candidate, a message was sent to "the Railsplitter" down in Springfield. Lincoln was busy playing baseball, and was interrupted to receive the news. History fails to record his performance in the game, but it was probably the last time he played.

A Most Interesting Conversation

Following World War II, Generals Dwight Eisenhower and Omar Bradley, and President Harry Truman were riding together in a procession in Berlin, Germany. Bradley saw Truman turn to Eisenhower and remark, "General, there is nothing that you may want that I won't try to help you get. That definitely and specifically includes the Presidency in 1948." Eisenhower laughed and said, "Mr. President, I don't know who your opponent will be for the Presidency, but it will not be I." Eisenhower kept his promise but did support Truman's opponent, Thomas Dewey, in 1948. President Truman might have kept his pledge had Eisenhower decided on becoming a Democrat.

Thanks, But No Thanks

After a long ride to Baltimore, Vice President Thomas Jefferson entered a hotel where a room had been reserved for him. Mr. Boydon, the hotel owner, had never met Jefferson and surveyed the dusty, dirty newcomer carefully. Convinced he was just a farmer, Boydon announced, "We have no room for you, sir." Not having heard the remark, Jefferson asked for a room, and was again rebuffed by the owner. The Vice President left and went a couple blocks to another hotel. Upon learning the identity of Jefferson, Boydon sent servants to apologize and bring him back. After he was located and presented a note of apology, Jefferson informed the messengers, "Tell him I have engaged a room. Tell Mr. Boydon that I value his good intentions highly, but if he has no room for a dirty farmer he shall have none for the Vice President."

You Know What I Mean

During the 1980 Presidential campaign, candidate Jimmy Carter stopped in Grand Rapids, Michigan to give a speech. It was later that he realized he had called it "Cedar Rapids." When Republican Gerald Ford publicly chided Carter for the slip, he shouted to the televison cameras that apparently Carter didn't even know Michigan was "one of the forty-eight states." For the next two days Ford tried to convince news reporters he knew there were *fifty* states.

Glad to See You Go

Not everyone it seems admired George Washington as President. As our nation's first leader, he took strong measures to institute his policies and enforce federal laws, often restricting the freedom of individuals or institutions. When George left office, one newspaper, the *Philadelphia Aurora,* stated in an editorial, "If ever there was a period for rejoicing, it is this moment." After serving his country for so long, perhaps even the first President agreed.

Orders for the Boss

After Gerald Ford's dog, Liberty, gave birth to nine puppies, First Lady Betty Ford would not allow photographs to be taken, fearing their eyes might be damaged from flash bulbs. She protected the pups' lungs too, and posted a sign above the door, saying, "No smoking, and this means you, grandpa." The warning was posted above a sketch of Gerald Ford with his pipe.

Bible Whiz

According to her son, Dwight, Ida Stover Eisenhower once won a prize for memorizing 1365 verses of the Bible. A pacifist, she was a Jehovah's Witness and a devoutly religious woman, but she seems to have had little influence on her son's views on war.

He Forgot Something

During battery practice one day, a young army officer prepared to fire a cannon. In his haste, however, the soldier forgot to unharness the mule attached to the cannon. When the fuse was lit, the frightened animal turned around. The big gun shot off in the opposite direction, partially destroying the house of a superior. Needless to say, the young officer was reprimanded. His name was U. S. Grant, and perhaps, this is why he was never an artillery officer.

I Won't Miss This Place

Benjamin Harrison did not enjoy his one term in office. During his administration the nation experienced bad economic times. Furthermore, there was a violent steel strike, the Johnstown Flood killed more than 2400 people in Pennsylvania, and the massacre of Indians took place at Wounded Knee, South Dakota, along with several other infamous incidents. The people tended to blame these events on the twenty-third President, though he had little or no control over them. In referring to the Executive Mansion, Harrison said, "There is my prison."

A Tale Written in Blood

William McKinley always wore a red carnation for good luck. Even as governor and congressman he wore a new one each day. Rarely did he remove it, even upon request. But in

September of 1901, a little girl asked the President if she might have the carnation he was wearing. He removed the flower from his lapel and gave it to her. A minute later, he was shot by a man in the reception line and died eight days later. Ohio, McKinley's home state, adopted the scarlet carnation as an official symbol. Each year, on McKinley's birthday, 535 Representatives and U. S. Senators are given red carnations in memory of our twenty-fifth President.

Indian Giver

In 1885 President Cleveland returned some of the Indian lands which his predecessor, Chester Arthur, had taken from some of the western tribes. Three years later, Cleveland reported to Congress that "over 80,000,000 acres have been arrested from illegal usurpation, improvident grants, and fraudulent entries and claims to be taken for the homesteads of honest industry." In spite of these efforts, Indian lands were eventually taken away.

Is That So?

A week before James K. Polk died, he fulfilled a long-standing promise to his wife and was baptized.

FDR loved to tell friends the true story of a foreign diplomat's wife who lost her panties as she was about to shake his hand at the White House.

Billy Carter's allergy to peanuts often kept him away from his brother, the President.

Not many things escaped the watchful eye of President Richard Nixon when it came to ceremonies. His 1972 inaugural parade was made pigeon-proof when Pennsylvania Avenue was sprayed with a chemical to keep the birds away.

According to at least one servant at the White House, Harry Truman washed his own underwear.

While attending the funeral of France's president George Pompidou, Nixon remarked before a group of people, "This is a great day for France."

While serving in prison for the assassination

of James A. Garfield, Charles Guiteau received hundreds of letters and telegrams each day congratulating him for shooting the President.

When Martin Van Buren was Vice President, he presided over the U.S. Senate with a pair of loaded pistols. In the decades preceding the Civil War there were frequent outbursts of violence in and around the Capitol.

Because of his obesity, John Adams was privately referred to as "His Rotundity" by members of Congress.

FDR's birthday, January 30, is a legal holiday in the Virgin Islands.

First Lady Rosalynn Carter's actual first name is Eleanor.

Even though FDR was elected President four times, he failed to carry his home county of Dutchess, New York in any of the four elections.

A President of the United States cannot be arrested without his consent.

Only two Presidents, Polk and Wilson, were elected without winning their home state.

Former heavyweight boxing champ Jack Dempsey, and President Franklin Roosevelt, once gave one of Dempsey's friends a "hot foot" in the Oval Office of the White House. FDR loved practical jokes.

One day while standing in the Oval Office, Harry Truman noticed the eagle in the Presidential Seal had its head pointed to the cluster of arrows instead of the olive branch. Truman quickly had it changed with the eagle looking the other way.

The furthest west George Washington ever traveled was to the present-day site of Pomeroy, Ohio, located in the southeast part of the state just across the Ohio River. He made this journey as a young officer prior to the Revolutionary War.

During the Great Depression and World War II, actor Ronald Reagan was a strong supporter of FDR and the New Deal programs. By the 1960's he had changed his political views.

On three separate occasions, President Richard Nixon gave Soviet Premier Leonid Brezhnev a new Cadillac, a Lincoln Continental, and a Chevrolet Monte Carlo. All three cars were donated by auto manufacturers. In turn, Nixon received a silver tea set, a painting of Moscow and a set of jewelry.

According to two European polls conducted in 1981, Ronald Reagan was one of the two most hated and feared men in history. Also ranking high were Adolph Hitler, Leonid Brezhnev, the Yorkshire Ripper and Muammar al-Qaddafi. A little unfair to the 40th President!

As chairman of the bonfire committee at Whittier College, Richard Nixon was given a difficult assignment. He was ordered to locate an outhouse with more than two compartments. The future President went above and beyond the call of duty, finding a "four seater," and adding it to the large blaze.

Only two Presidents had signatures with upright letters—John Quincy Adams and Lyndon B. Johnson. All the rest signed their names with slanted letters.

Eisenhower believed his Secretary of State had been born for the job. John Foster Dulles was well-equipped for this important post. In addition to his wide experience, Dulles was a scholarly genius. His father was Secretary of State under Benjamin Harrison, and his uncle, Robert Lansing, served in that capacity for Woodrow Wilson. Dulles proved to be a strong, forceful and courageous statesman, dying of cancer during Eisenhower's second term.

William Howard Taft once remarked, "It seems to be the profession of a President simply to hear other people talk."

Five U. S. Presidents purchased no china dinnerware during their terms in office. They were Andrew Johnson, William Taft, Warren Harding, Calvin Coolidge and Herbert Hoover. All Republicans, and all trying to make cuts in spending.

It was Herbert Hoover who said, "All men are equal before fish."

Eleanor Roosevelt's name was Rover! This was the code name assigned to her during the days of World War II when she made extensive trips for the President. FDR often referred to his wife as his "eyes and legs."

Thirteen Presidents have also served as Vice President of the U. S.

George Washington and James Madison are the only Presidents whose signatures are on the Constitution.

Calvin Coolidge was a man of very few words. It was said he could remain silent in six different languages, and when writer Dorothy Parker was told the ex-President was dead, she asked, "How do you know?" Many stories, some of them untrue, demonstrate Coolidge's silence.

A dozen Presidents were army generals. And though an admiral has never become President, five Chief Executives have served in the navy.

Six Presidents had the first name of James.

Three Presidents attended college but did not graduate: Monroe, William Harrison and McKinley.

It was only after four years of courting his future bride that John Tyler got up enough nerve to kiss her hand!

Lyndon B. Johnson said there was a distinct advantage in having all the members of his family with the same initials of L. B. J. Said the President, "It's cheaper this way because we can all use the same luggage."

James Garfield did not think much of inauguration ceremonies. He once suggested that the outgoing President be brought before the new one and executed by a firing squad. Now *that* would really liven things up!

Woodrow Wilson was the only one of our Presidents to *earn* a Ph. D.

Grant's wife, Julia, was cross-eyed. He refused to have this affliction corrected because he like her the way she was.

The Baby Ruth candy bar was not named for Babe Ruth, the Yankee outfielder. It was named in honor of Ruth Cleveland, born October 3, 1891. Daughter of President Grover Cleveland, she died in her teens in 1904. It is made by the Curtiss Candy Company.

No President was an only child.

Two Presidents had fathers who were blacksmiths: Abe Lincoln and Herbert Hoover.

The only President to attain his 33rd degree Mason was Harry Truman. Warren Harding had been nominated but died before receiving it.

A total of eight Johnsons, five Smiths and four Kings have run for President or Vice President at one time or another.

Woodrow Wilson was the only President to have *two* daughters married in the White House.

A total of 18 Presidents also served as governors (two of these were governors of territories). Sixteen others never served in Congress.

A total of 85 sons have been born to Presidents, and just 59 daughters. The "Grand Prize," however, for the most grandchildren goes to William Henry Harrison. "Old Tippecanoe" had 48 grandchildren and 106 great grandchildren.

John Quincy Adams was also the first U. S. Ambassador to Russia.

Six Presidents married widows, including three of the first four.

Which President was a once a cook in the U. S. Army? None other than William McKinley. The young Ohioan was promoted rapidly because of numerous acts of courage while his regiment was under fire. Incidentally, McKinley's commander was another future President, Rutherford B. Hayes.

FDR vetoed 631 congressional bills, but one should remember he was elected four times. Grover Cleveland, who served two terms, "axed" 584 bills. These are the most vetoes by any two Presidents.

Three Presidents were sons of ministers—or PK's (preacher's kids). Five Chief Magistrates married daughters of ministers. Woodrow Wilson, son of a minister, also married the daughter of one. Nothing like keeping it in the family.

The oldest tree on the White House lawn is a great American elm, planted in 1826 by John Quincy Adams. And it's still growing!

When James K. Polk ran for President in 1844, he was accused of having branded his initials on the shoulders of 43 slaves. If there was truth to this statement, it did not affect the outcome of the election. Polk won.

The first movie Jimmy Carter saw in the White House was *All The President's Men.*

While residing at the Executive Mansion, Thomas Jefferson kept bears in a cage on the grounds.

John Kennedy graduated from Harvard, but when he was eighteen he was enrolled in another Ivy League school—Princeton. His freshman year was cut short by illness and he transferred to Harvard.

The cornerstone for the White House was laid in 1792. The first occupants of the new structure, John and Abigail Adams, found it empty and lonesome. The First Lady made good use of the available space by hanging her washing in the East Room.

Andrew Jackson was only thirteen years old when he was a soldier fighting against the British during the Revolutionary War. Jackson had a deep hatred for the English, and once was struck by a British officer's sword when he refused to shine the redcoat's boots. Other members of his family were imprisoned.

Harry Truman was a common man, and a humble one. He offered this advice to his successors: "The President hears a hundred voices telling him that he is the greatest man in the world. He must listen carefully indeed to hear the one voice that tells him he is not."

"Nobody can acquire honor by doing what is wrong." So said Thomas Jefferson.

When Alaska was purchased from Russia in 1868 it was dubbed "Seward's Folly" and "Seward's Ice Box" in "honor" of Andrew Johnson's Secretary of State, William Seward. Believed at the time to be a bad bargain, the press made certain the President himself did not escape criticism. Alaska was also called "Andy Johnson's Polar Bear Garden."

Mrs. Coolidge, in presiding over the Easter egg-rolling contest for children, exhibited her pet raccoon, Rebecca.

The first U. S. Senator to become President was James Monroe.

Calvin Coolidge was the first President sworn into office by a former President—William H. Taft, then Chief Justice of the U. S. Supreme Court.

Three Presidential families had children born in foreign countries: John Quincy Adams (a son born in Germany and a daughter in Russia), Herbert Hoover (two sons born in England), and Franklin Roosevelt (FDR Jr. was born in New Brunswick, Canada).

No President has ever died in the month of May.

More Presidents attended Harvard University than any other college. Six of our nation's leaders graduated from there; they were both Adamses, both Roosevelts, Rutherford B. Hayes and John Kennedy.

The oldest President to marry was Benjamin Harrison. Marrying for the second time, he wedded the 38-year-old niece of his deceased wife. He was 62 at the time and retired from public office.

Dwight Eisenhower had *two* oval offices in the White House. The official one was in the west wing; another one adjacent to it was sometimes used for important business. Eisenhower called it the Trophy Room.

The first Presidential mansion was at No. 1 Cherry Street in New York City, where George Washington resided for nearly a year.

The President of the United States must pay income tax.

Though much publicity has gone to the Hayeses for starting the Easter Roll on the White House lawn, this event actually began during the years when James and Dolley Madison occupied the Executive Mansion. Begun in 1813, it was held on the grounds near the Capitol Building. But when the British destroyed the government buildings that same year, the ritual was discontinued. After the Civil War, the nineteenth President and First Lady Lucy Hayes sponsored it once again. Not long ago, during Jerry Ford's term, plastic eggs were substituted, bringing forth cries of protest from farmers in the Washington, D. C. area. (Author's note: On the 100th anniversary of the White House Easter Egg Roll, my son, Matthew, won first prize. He received a blue ribbon and a letter of congratulations from Betty Ford. The race includes hundreds of children who compete in groups.)

James Madison and Zachary Taylor were second cousins.

Coolidge, like Jefferson and Teddy Roosevelt, was a great lover of pets. Among "Silent Cal's" lesser known animal friends were a pair of canaries named Nip and Tuck, a cat named Tiger, and a dog called Prudence Prim.

113

Warren G. Harding made the first radio broadcast by a U. S. President. That was in 1922.

Evidence shows that Andrew Jackson may have been born on board a ship bound from Ireland to the colonies. Jackson claimed he was born in South Carolina, thus making him eligible for the Presidency.

Gerald Ford was the only one of our Presidents to have earned an Eagle Scout Award.

Did you know one of our Presidents has his protrait on U. S. paper currency, and that it is rarely, if ever, seen? Woodrow Wilson is portrayed on the $100,000 bill. These large denomination notes have not been printed for decades, and are used exclusively among a couple U. S. banks as money exchanges.

All the Presidents up to Harry Truman paid not only for their own meals, but also for the meals of the staff and even guests. During the Truman administration, Congress appropriated funds to help the First Family feed guests and White House employees.

Gas pipes were installed in the White House in 1848 while James K. Polk was President.

No President has ever done a paid TV commercial while in office.

Herbert Hoover lived the longest amount of time after leaving the Oval Office. He lived to the ripe old age of 90, surviving his term nearly 32 years. John Adams, however, was the oldest living ex-President. He too was 90 years of age, besting Hoover by just a few days.

The name "White House" did not become official until Teddy Roosevelt had the title put on letterheads. The Executive Mansion was dubbed "White House" after layers of white paint were used to hide the black scars it received from the British during the War of 1812.

Woodrow Wilson kept lawn care costs down when he grazed sheep on the White House lawn during World War I. More than $100,000 was raised from the sale of "White House wool" and this money was donated to charities.

One of the more infamous Presidential edicts was Executive Order 9066. That is when FDR incarcerated Japanese-Americans in camps in 1942. 112,000 U. S. citizens, most of them living on the west coast, were affected.

Because of severe intestinal disorders, Thomas Jefferson and James K. Polk died from diarrhea.

Benjamin Harrison's daughter, Mary, born to his second wife, was younger than Harrison's four grandchildren.

When Theodore Roosevelt was inaugurated President in March of 1904 (his second term), he was presented a strange gift. John Hay, Secretary to President Lincoln, gave Teddy a ring made from Lincoln's hair. The lock of hair had been snipped from the dying President while he lay on his deathbed. Hay thought Roosevelt would be honored by wearing it, and he was.

Speaking of Teddy Roosevelt, he tried to have "In God We Trust" removed from U. S. coins and currency. Mr. Roosevelt had liberal views of the Almighty; he also believed the inscription was sacreligious and a violation of church and state separation.

FDR was related to eleven United States Presidents!

As you may have read, Ohio and Virginia have both been called the "Mother of Presidents," because eight Chief Executives have been born or raised in each of these states. But, do you know which state has given us the most First Ladies? It's New York, which has provided eight.

A total of 15 Presidents were Masons.

When Millard Fillmore was born, his mother feared the child was retarded.

William McKinley became bankrupt three years before his election to the White House. His debts of $200,000 were paid in part by his friend and political boss, Mark Hanna.

During Franklin Roosevelt's terms in office, his rail travel exceeded ten times the distance around the earth.

During his time in office, President Hoover never once attended the theater.

Chester Arthur once had a 14-course meal served to guests at the White House.

Lyndon B. Johnson's favorite soft drink was Fresca. He enjoyed it so much that a special tap was installed at the White House.

Jefferson had a plethora of inventions, among them the dumb-waiter, swivel chair and the folding bed.

James A. Garfield was the first President to have his mother live in the Executive Mansion. "Grandma" Garfield was not impressed by the experience. A pioneer woman, she felt Washington society was too strenuous. She preferred doing the washing than attending a party.

Every school student knows that Alexander

Hamilton was killed by Aaron Burr in a gun duel. Hamilton, however, had challenged another man, but both men were persuaded not to carry it through. That *other* man was a future President—his name was James Monroe.

As a young man this future President contemplated suicide, and was advised by a friend not to carry his pocket knife. After losing his job as a clerk, and failing at several other vocations, he lost an appointment as a land commissioner. Later he lost a bid for his party's choice as a vice presidential candidate; this followed being voted out of his congressional seat. Later in his career he lost two races for the Senate. And one of the main reasons he was nominated for President was because he was the least known of the candidates. His name was Abraham Lincoln.

Benjamin Harrison was the last President who wore a beard in public.

During their terms in office, both Presidents Grant and Lyndon Johnson were stopped for speeding by police. Grant was "nabbed" in a carriage in Washington, D. C., and LBJ was stopped on a Texas highway.

Benjamin Harrison gave 140 speeches in 30 days and all of them were different. Possessing a fine legal mind and a keen ability for public speaking, the President performed this feat during an official tour of the Pacific Coast.

Robert Lincoln lost his father's inaugural speech enroute from Springfield, Illinois to the Capitol. Papa Lincoln finally located it in a sack in the train's baggage car.

Thomas Jefferson knew six other languages besides English.

Theodore Roosevelt shaved every day at 12:40 p.m.

George Washington had a pair of false teeth carved from rhinoceros ivory. He also had wooden ones made. A pair of his ivory teeth were exhibited at the Chicago World's Fair in 1933.

Lincoln contracted smallpox during his Presidency and was confined to bed for several weeks.

Andrew Jackson once had his nose twisted by an irate office seeker.

Born with a distinct speech impediment—a lisp, Tad Lincoln, the President's youngest son, was a real rascal, often interrupting his father during important meetings. He once blasted open a White House door with a toy cannon. And when he wasn't busy chasing his pet turkey, "Jack," the youngster often hid in his father's office, only to "attack" those who visited with the sixteenth President.

John F. Kennedy once described Washington, D. C. as a city of "northern charm and southern efficiency." He was, however, somewhat critical of his fellow members of Congress in 1946 when he remarked, "The House is run by a crowd of old men who would have been pensioned off years ago if they were in private industry."

For several years, First Lady Grace Coolidge was considered as the "Number One Fan" of the Boston Red Sox.

INNING	1	2	3	4	5	6	7	8	9	
BOSTON	0	0	0	0	0	0	0	0	0	O
CLEVE.	0	1	2	0	3	2	1	4	0	13

DARN THOSE SOX! BUT I STILL LOVE 'EM.

U. S. Grant had the coldest inauguration. On the day of his second inauguration in 1873, it was 4 degrees above zero with a fierce wind blowing.

John Tyler had to borrow money from a friend so he could be sworn in as President in 1841.

February 14, 1884 was a Valentine's Day Theodore Roosevelt would always remember. On that day his first wife, Alice, and his mother both died in the same house. He married his second wife, Edith, in 1886.

The first movie ever shown in the White House was D. W. Griffith's classic, "The Birth of a Nation." President Wilson watched it in 1916.

A life-size statue was cast of Warren G. Harding's dog, Laddie Boy. After Harding's death in 1923, the newsboys across the country collected pennies in honor of Harding, who had been a newspaper publisher in Marion, Ohio. The 19,134 pennies were melted down and molded into a statue that is now in the Smithsonian Institution.

When he was elected President, Ulysses S. Grant said to his wife, "Well, I'm sorry to have to tell you, but I guess they've elected me."

At one time James K. Polk, Martin Van Buren and Frank Pierce all lived in the same Washington, D. C. boarding house. A frequent guest of these three men was Francis Scott Key, who penned the immortal lines of the "Star Spangled Banner."

Lucy Hayes loved children. Every year she gave special parties for the children of the White House staff. She also sent gifts daily to a Washington children's hospital.

Andrew Jackson often wore two pairs of eye glasses at the same time. While using one pair for reading, another pair, perched on his forehead, was used for looking at distant objects.

One observer at James Buchanan's inauguration noted the new President "sighed audibly and frequently."

U. S. Supreme Court Justice Brewer once remarked about "Big Bill" Taft's manners, "Taft is the politest man in Washington; the other day he gave up his seat in a street car to three ladies!"

One evening at dinner, President Harry Truman and his wife, Bess, squirted watermelon seeds at each other.

Eliza Johnson, the wife of our 17th President, made only one public appearance during her husband's term. This was in celebration of Andy's 60th birthday. Mrs. Johnson was an invalid.

John F. Kennedy was the first President to have been a Boy Scout.

Dolley Madison was the first hostess to serve ice cream in the White House. She was often referred to as "The Lady Presidentress."

In Frankfurt, Germany, just after World War II, General Dwight Eisenhower told a group of people, "We are going to have peace even if we have to fight for it."

U. S. Grant said, "Labor disgraces no man. Unfortunately, man often disgraces labor."

Rutherford B. Hayes said, "He serves his party best who serves his country best."

Andrew Jackson was the first President to have a Cabinet appointee rejected by the U. S. Senate when he nominated Roger B. Taney for Secretary of the Treasury in 1834. It was a blessing in disguise for Taney, who later was named Chief Justice of the U. S. Supreme Court.

Our nation doubled in size when Jefferson purchased the Louisiana Territory in 1803. The cost? About 4¢ an acre, or $16,000,000. Not a bad bargain when one considers we were only supposed to buy New Orleans; Napoleon of France, however, needed the money to finance his war and he unloaded the entire region.

FDR was the first President to make a radio broadcast in a foreign language. During World War II he spoke via the radio to the people of France.

Herbert Hoover, born on August 10, 1874, was the first President born west of the Missssippi River. He was born in West Branch, Iowa.

Twenty-five of our Chief Executives were lawyers. No doubt many of the others were "admitted to bars" too!

President Richard Nixon once demonstrated his yoyo techniques with country-western singer, Roy Acuff, at the Grand Ole Opry in Nashville.

"Duty determines destiny." So said William McKinley.

President Chester A. Arthur designed the Presidential Flag.

Presidents Taylor, Grant, Garfield, Taft, Coolidge and Kennedy all smoked cigars—and Woodrow Wilson was said to have chewed tobacco.

It cost the U. S. government $100 to embalm the body of Abraham Lincoln.

George Washington was a man of immense physical strength. He crushed walnuts with one hand. He was also a man of exquisite taste; at his second inauguration he dressed in black velvet with diamond knee buckles.

Lou Hoover was head of the Girl Scouts, and increased their membership from 200,000 to nearly a million in just three years.

A statue at the U. S. Naval Academy in Annapolis, Md., honors the military service of Chester A. Arthur's father-in-law. And aren't you just dying to know what that service was?!

Upon leaving the Executive Mansion for the last time, John Adams returned home to Quincy, Massachusetts, where he discovered a large amount of fertilizer for his farm. The second President was quite happy, remarking he had made a good exchange of "honors and virtues for manure."

Thomas Jefferson manufacured nails. This was in 1796 and 1797 while he lived at Monticello.

Warren Harding was the first President to visit Alaska.

When Andrew Jackson died in 1845 his pet parrot had to be removed during the funeral service because of its profanity, no doubt taught to him by its master.

Abe Lincoln pardoned many prisoners and soldiers who had been charged with cowardice or desertion. Concerning one pardon, he wrote, "I think this boy can do more good above ground than under."

Frank Pierce's father was among the small group of minutemen who fought against the British at Lexington and Concord in 1775. Papa Pierce thus witnessed the "shot heard 'round the world."

President Andrew Johnson never attended school—not even a single day. His predecessor, Lincoln, attended school only five months.

John Adams wore a sword while presiding over the U. S. Senate during his term as Vice President.

Abraham Lincoln truly deserved the title "Honest Abe." During his congressional campaign the Whig Party gave him $200, and he returned $199.25. As he explained, "You see, I didn't need it all." The 75¢ was spent on a barrel of cider to treat some farmers.

George Washington's brother was married five times.

Supreme Court Justice Oliver Wendell Holmes once publicly greeted President Rutherford B. Hayes as "His Honesty, The President."

"Teaching school was the hardest job I ever had," said our twenty-ninth President, Warren G. Harding.

In 1964 Columbia University selected Thomas Edison, and one other American, as the two greatest engineers in American history. That *other* American also happened to be a U. S. President; his name was Herbert Hoover.

Emily Spinach once lived in the White House. This was the name of Alice Roosevelt's pet garter snake when her papa, Theodore, was President.

Andrew Johnson was the youngest of the Presidents to have fathered a child. Young dad was just nineteen.

The first Japanese delegation ever sent to the United States was during the one term of James Buchanan.

James Madison was the "best farmer in the world." So said Thomas Jefferson, who was quite a farmer himself.

Eisenhower once said, "If all Americans want is security, they can go to prison."

Water was first piped into the White House during Andrew Jackson's administration.

It is believed John Quincy Adams proposed the first toast at a formal dinner in the White House. This was done on September 6, 1825, when Lafayette was a guest of honor. It was the Frenchman's birthday.

Coolidge was the first President to use a radio in rescuing an animal. When his pet cat, Tiger, was discovered missing, he sent out a plea for help. Tiger was found with a "mate" near the Navy Department Building.

James Buchanan was our only bachelor President.

The Tomb of the Unknown Soldier and the Lincoln Memorial were both dedicated by President Warren G. Harding.

When Theodore Roosevelt was asked to comment on the nomination of Warren Harding to the U. S. Senate, the former President had nothing to say, "No, not one word."

Thomas Jefferson personally wrote more than 25,000 letters during his lifetime. Teddy Roosevelt was also a prolific letter writer.

James K. Polk once adjourned a cabinet meeting to meet the famous dwarf, Tom Thumb.

John Quincy Adams installed the first billiard table in the White House.

No President whose last name began with the letter "H" was ever re-elected. We've had five of them.

After leaving the Presidency, Thomas Jefferson was $20,000 in debt—a hefty sum in those days. He could balance the federal budget but couldn't pay his private debts.

Many historians regard William McKinley as the most friendly President.

Lincoln's body lay in state in 14 different cities.

Just before the attack on Pearl Harbor, Franklin Roosevelt purchased a book entitled, *Exploration in the South Pacific*.

Lincoln never delivered his famous speech at Gettysburg! When Lincoln dedicated the battlefield as a national cemetery in November of 1863, his two and one-half minute address took place in Cumberland Township, outside of the borough of Gettysburg. Newspaper accounts, incidentally, were highly critical of Lincoln's remarks. It is also interesting that photographer Mathew Brady waited for three hours to get a picture of Lincoln delivering the Gettysburg Address. He went to his wagon to get a cup of coffee while two other speakers gave long orations, and by the time Brady got back, the President had already given his speech and sat down.

Rutherford B. Hayes, also known as "Rudd," was the first President married to a college graduate. His wife, Lucy, graduated with honors from Wesleyan College. During the Civil War, Hayes distinguished himself in battle while Lucy worked for a brief spell as a nurse.

The last bearded President was not Benjamin Harrison; it was Woodrow Wilson! While recovering from a stroke, the bedridden Chief Executive grew a long grey beard. When he finally did appear in public after several months, he emerged clean shaven.

In My Opinion

The ten Presidents who vacationed the most during their administrations:

1. Calvin Coolidge
2. Ulysses S. Grant
3. Chester Arthur
4. Dwight D. Eisenhower
5. Franklin D. Roosevelt
6. Richard Nixon
7. John F. Kennedy
8. Warren Harding
9. Jimmy Carter
10. Ronald Reagan

Note: Twentieth century Presidents need a vacation.

The ten hardest-working Presidents:

1. James K. Polk
2. George Washington
3. Abraham Lincoln
4. Franklin D. Roosevelt
5. Grover Cleveland
6. John Adams
7. Theodore Roosevelt
8. Thomas Jefferson

9. Harry Truman
10. James Madison
    Andrew Jackson

The ten weakest Presidents (based upon leadership qualities, political influence, achievements, lack of communication, etc.):

1. Ulysses S. Grant
2. Warren Harding
3. Millard Fillmore
4. James Buchanan
5. Franklin Pierce
6. Chester Arthur
7. Andrew Johnson
8. Richard Nixon
9. Benjamin Harrison
10. Martin Van Buren

The ten Presidents with the worst luck (based upon loss in family, personal illness or injury, a poor economy, inefficiency, misunderstandings, etc.):

1. Herbert Hoover
2. Franklin Pierce
3. Andrew Johnson
4. Zachary Taylor
5. Richard Nixon
6. Martin Van Buren

7. John Tyler
8. Jimmy Carter
9. William McKinley
10. William Henry Harrison
    James A. Garfield
    Abraham Lincoln

The ten most intelligent Presidents (based upon education, intellectual capacity, literary achievement, etc.):

1. Thomas Jefferson
2. John Quincy Adams
3. James A. Garfield
4. Woodrow Wilson
5. Herbert Hoover
6. John Adams
7. Theodore Roosevelt
8. Chester Arthur
9. William H. Taft
10. John Kennedy
    James Buchanan

Answers

1. Jimmy Carter. All the rest, including Reagan, were born at home.

2. Scorpio or Aquarius. Five Presidents were born under each sign.

3. Ulysses S. Grant.

4. William Howard Taft.

5. Benjamin Harrison, grandson of President William Henry Harrison.

6. Rutherford B. Hayes. Due to a disputed election in 1876, there was some concern that his opponent, Samuel Tilden, would be named. Hayes took his oath of office on a Sunday, and then publicly the next day. Grant, his predecessor, had his term expire on a Saturday and worried politicians did not want to have any day without a President.

7. Ronald Reagan at 69 years old, besting William Henry Harrison by one year.

8. Warren G. Harding, our 29th President.

9. Abraham Lincoln. I'm sure we would all like to see more of him!

10. James A. Garfield.

11. Dwight D. Eisenhower.

12. Theodore Roosevelt in 1870, while accompanying his family on a European tour.

13. This one is difficult to answer. It was probably John Tyler (10th President) or James K. Polk (11th President). A photograph of William Henry Harrison does exist, but it was probably taken just prior to his inauguration when he visited New York, where the camera had just been introduced into the United States in 1840. Presidents John Quincy Adams, Andrew Jackson, and Martin Van Buren all had a daguerreotype taken after they left office.

14. Our 15th President James Buchanan when he and his cabinet posed for Mathew Brady in March of 1857.

15. That same man—Benjamin Harrison, our 23rd President. Let's face it; Harrison had "trying times" in the outdoors!

16. Virginia and Ohio. Ironically, both states claim William Henry Harrison as their favorite son. He was born in Virginia but moved to Ohio at a very early age. Indiana also claims this same Harrison, since he lived there for a while and served as its territorial governor.

17. William Howard Taft, who stood at 6' 3" and weighed at times 345 pounds. And remember, people in 1909 were generally smaller than Americans of today, and furniture was built accordingly.

18. James Garfield, born in 1831 in northeastern Ohio.

19. That same man—James Garfield, in the 1880 elections.

20. William McKinley, our 25th President. As a young man, Bill served in the Union Army, beginning as a private and later being decorated for bravery and becoming an officer.

21. James Garfield and William McKinley. Though Garfield was shot in the back by Charles Guiteau, the assassin had previously had two job interviews with the 20th President. Leon Czolgoz shot McKinley in the stomach as he was shak-

ing hands with him at the Pan American Exposition in Buffalo, New York in 1901.

22. Yes. Three First Ladies died; they were the wives of Benjamin Harrison, John Tyler, and Woodrow Wilson. Tyler and Wilson remarried while in office.

23. Sarah Polk, who died in 1891, lived 42 years after the 11th President died. Francis Cleveland, married to the President when she was 21, survived her husband almost 40 years. On the other hand, Abigail Fillmore died just a few days after the 13th President left office.

24. President James K. Polk, who passed away just three months after leaving office. He was mentally and physically exhausted and in poor health.

25. Grover Cleveland, whose young and beautiful wife even issued a statement charging the Republicans that their allegation was "a foolish campaign story without a shadow of foundation." Cleveland lost the 1888 election but returned to the White House four years later, becoming the only man to serve two non-consecutive terms. The main reason for his defeat in 1888 was his uncompromising stand on the tariff issue.

26. Andrew Jackson, whose intended assassin, Richard Lawrence, walked up to him and aimed two pistols. Both guns malfunctioned and "Old Hickory" was given a "new lease on life."

27. John F. Kennedy. Grant's parents were both alive when he took office, but his mother did not attend because, according to some sources, she did not receive a formal invitation.

28. A-8, B-2, C-6, D-7, E-5, F-4, G-3, H-1.

29. Woodrow Wilson, while in Milan, Italy. As the huge crowd listened to patriotic American tunes, the 28th President conducted the music.

30. True. This happened while he was on one of his hunting expeditions and captured two cubs. The press was there to take pictures and an adoring public later bought toy stuffed bears which, to this day, are still called teddy bears. One of the bears, incidentally, is preserved and located in the Smithsonian Institution.

31. George Washington and Thomas Jefferson.

32. Warren G. Harding. He should have listened.

33. Texan Jack Garner, who kindly referred that way to Franklin Roosevelt.

34. Mrs. Garfield. Garfield's father died
when James was two years old while he
was fighting a forest fire near their log
cabin.

35. Franklin Pierce. The Vice President-
Elect, William King, was ill with tuber-
culosis in Cuba and died just a month
after taking his oath in absentia. King
was the only one of all the Presidents
and Vice Presidents to take his oath of
office in a foreign country.

36. John Tyler, who took office after Harrison's unexpected death in 1841. Tyler,
a Whig, insisted upon being addressed
as "Mr. President."

37. A-3, B-1, C-9, D-4, E-6, F-7, G-8, H-10,
I-5, J-11, K-2.

38. True. It happened while T. R. was
visiting Nashville, Tennessee.

39. After the first three outs in the top of
the seventh inning, Taft rose to "loosen
up" his large frame. Out of respect for
the President, the fans also got up out
of their seats, thinking he was leaving
the ball park. The President sat down

and so did the spectators. Thus began the seventh inning stretch.

40. John Tyler—15. Tyler's first wife died while he was in office, and he remarried Julia Gardiner, who bore him five sons and two daughters. Letitia Christian, his first wife, bore eight children before she died in 1842.

41. James K. Polk, who often put in 20-hour days at his job.

42. Yes, six of them: Washington (French and Indian War, surface wound), Monroe (Revolutionary War), Grant, Hayes (Civil War), Theodore Roosevelt (slightly wounded in Spanish-American War) and Kennedy (World War II). Taylor, Pierce, Garfield and Eisenhower were also injured but not directly due to enemy gunfire.

43. William Henry Harrison who, in March of 1841, spoke for nearly two hours (over 8000 words) in a cold and damp Washington. Harrison did not wear any hat or overcoat. He caught a cold, developed chills, and died from pneumonia just a month later.

44. The same man, William Henry Harrison, who fought in the French and Indian War.

45. Theodore Roosevelt, 42 years of age, besting John Kennedy by a few months.

46. A Southerner, John Breckenridge, served under James Buchanan at the age of 36.

47. Records show it was played by the Marine Band for Martin Van Buren. Published in 1810, it may have been played before that.

48. George Washington's second inaugural address of 135 words lasted about four minutes. Franklin D. Roosevelt had the next shortest, a six-minute speech on January 20, 1945, at Andrews Air Force Base. Technically, Lyndon Johnson's 57-word address, following Kennedy's assassination, was the briefest. This ceremony, however, was not preplanned like regular inaugurations.

49. James Madison, who donned all-Yankee garb on March 4, 1809.

50. Sunday, March 4, 1849, between James Polk and incoming Zachary Taylor, who was sworn in the next day.

51. Zachary Taylor, whose daughter Knox eloped with Jefferson Davis, later President of the Confederate States of

America. She died three months after the marriage, and Taylor and Davis did not speak to one another for ten years. Davis later remarried.

52. This was the first time the entire country voted for a President on the same day.

53. John Tyler of Virginia. His cabinet suggested he be addressed as "Vice President," but Tyler insisted upon being called "President" after Harrison's death in 1841. Daniel Webster, his Secretary of State, stayed on throughout most of the term.

54. William Harrison's papa, Benjamin.

55. George Washington, first in New York and then in Philadelphia four years later.

56. A-2, B 1, C-9, D-11, E-3, F-6, G-7, H-4, I-8, J-10, K-5.

57. Franklin D. Roosevelt's pet, Fala, at the third inauguration.

58. Gerald R. Ford, born in Omaha. He later moved to Michigan. His original name was Leslie King, Jr.

59. Dwight D. Eisenhower, who moved to Kansas at a young age.

60. John Adams and his wife Abigail, while looking for the newly constructed Washington City in November of 1800.

61. John Quincy Adams in 1825.

62. On Sunday, March 4, 1821, John Gaillard of South Carolina, President Pro Tem of the Senate, assumed the Presidency for one day between James Monroe's two terms.

63. Thomas Jefferson, sworn in by John Marshall, who was appointed Chief Justice by the previous President, John Adams.

64. Ronald Reagan. Abraham Lincoln was born near Hodgensville, Kentucky, in 1809, though he is often considered a native son of Illinois.

65. Abraham Lincoln, both in 1860 and 1864, when the southern states were in rebellion.

66. Depending on one's perspective, this may be true. More than a dozen Chief

Executives have had attempts on their lives, and four others have died either during or shortly after their stay in office. Pertaining to normal jobs, however, firemen, sanitation and construction workers, chemical workers, policemen, lumberjacks, and coal miners rank respectively according to surveys.

67. Franklin D. Roosevelt, when he made Frances Perkins his Secretary of Labor. She was in office from 1933 to 1945.

68. Millard Fillmore.

69. Woodrow Wilson and Theodore Roosevelt.

70. Zachary Taylor. His son, incidentally, was a Confederate general during the War Between the States.

71. A-4, B-3, C-1, D-2. Grant later changed his name from Hiram Ulysses to Ulysses Simpson, because he didn't like being teased about having the initials H.U.G.

72. 72 years.

73. Calvin Coolidge in 1872.

74. Ulysses S. Grant, who, in 1872, earned $25,000, and had it doubled at the beginning of his second term. What a pay raise!

75. Andrew Jackson in 1833.

76. They were: John and Abigail Adams, Thomas Jefferson, Abraham and Mary Lincoln, Calvin and Grace Coolidge, and John and Jacqueline Kennedy.

77. Rutherford Hayes' son, Webb, for gallant action in the Philippines during the Spanish-American War in 1899; and Theodore Roosevelt, Jr. for bravery on June 6, 1944 (D-Day) during the Normandy Invasion.

78. Andrew Johnson, a tailor, made his own clothes. Tricky, eh?

79. Lyndon B. Johnson, when he appointed Robert Weaver as Secretary of Housing and Urban Development.

80. Woodrow Wilson, following World War I.

81. George Washington, on April 30, 1789. A statue of him is there today.

82. James Monroe. Monrovia, Liberia is located in west Africa. Only blacks may become citizens, and Monroe was a slave owner (though a benevolent one).

83. D. Kennedy did smoke cigars, usually in private. Grant and Garfield smoked cigars regularly.

84. D.

85. C. Millard Fillmore turned the honor down, explaining he had never done anything to deserve it.

86. C. Grover Cleveland's second daughter, Esther, was born there in 1893.

87. A. The other couple celebrating 25 years of marriage while in the White House were the Tafts.

88. B. This was done at the request of President Warren Harding.

89. C.

90. D. James Madison weighed only 100 pounds—with his clothes on!

91. A. Andrew Johnson in 1867 entertain-

ed Queen Emma of the Sandwich Islands. Ulysses Grant entertained King David of Hawaii in 1874 and Emperor Don Pedro of Brazil in 1876.

92. C.

93. C. Thomas Jefferson, former governor of Virginia.

94. A.

95. William Howard Taft.

96. Dwight D. Eisenhower.

97. The President's father, David.

98. This was said by Woodrow Wilson's second wife, Edith, after he had suffered a stroke, and quoted to a group of officials who demanded to see the stricken Chief Executive.

99. Dwight D. Eisenhower.

100. Dwight D. Eisenhower.

101. Dwight D. Eisenhower.

102. Episcopalian. Nine of them were

Episcopalians and seven were Presbyterians.

103. It is due to the sum of the numbers in 1776, the year of our nation's birth.

104. Quincy, Massachusetts, the home of John and John Quincy Adams.

105. William Taft, who served from 1909 to 1912.

106. George Washington, when he appointed Alexander Hamilton as his Secretary of the Treasury in 1789.

107. William McKinley, at his first inauguration on March 4, 1897.

108. Zachary Taylor or Dwight Eisenhower. Taylor served in the War of 1812, the Black Hawk War and Seminole Uprising of the 1830's, and the Mexican War. "Ike" was the allied commander in World War II, after having served in World War I. He also played a small role in the Korean War.

109. Calvin Coolidge. Incidentally, Jefferson and Tyler played the violin. Harding played the cornet, and Truman and Nixon played the piano.

110. Theodore Roosevelt, who was submerged about 30 feet.

111. Lucy Webb Hayes, graduating with highest honors from Wesleyan College in Cincinnati in 1852.

112. Grover Cleveland, who moved to New York as a youngster.

113. Benjamin Harrison, who served between the two non-consecutive terms of Grover Cleveland.

114. Richard Nixon in 1974.

115. Martha Washington, who was given franking privilege in 1800.

116. Grover Cleveland. While President, he had a cancerous growth removed from his mouth. Economic conditions in the summer of 1893 were very bad, and no one close to the President dared to let the media or public know that the Chief Executive needed major surgery. To avoid publicity, the operation was performed on the President's yacht as it cruised the waters of New York, giving the impression that Cleveland was on a fishing venture. The surgery lasted only a half hour, but it took Cleveland several days to recover. Thus, the stock

market was spared the discouraging news.

117. John Quincy Adams was the youngest and oldest public servant; at age 14, he was a secretary to the U.S. Ambassador to Russia. Later he served in the U.S. Congress, following his term as President. He died while serving there at the age of 80.

118. Ronald Reagan in 1982. In a week's time, he received 19 train sets as gifts, giving most of them away.

119. Abraham Lincoln (Robert Lincoln), James Garfield (James Garfield, Jr.), Herbert Hoover (Herbert Hoover, Jr.), and Franklin D. Roosevelt (Franklin D. Roosevelt, Jr.).

120. Richard Nixon, who witnessed the launch of Apollo 12 in 1969.

121. Richard Nixon in 1972. In a huge landslide, he defeated everyone, including Democrat George McGovern, capturing 49 of the 50 states. Incidentally, there were about 11,000 write-in votes in the '72 election.

122. Thomas Jefferson. Washington and

Adams, his predecessors, bowed instead of shaking hands.

123. John Tyler, who, at the time of his death in 1862, had been elected as a Confederate congressman. The United States government made no mention of his death. Only 50 years after his death did Congress authorize a monument for him.

124. They were all teachers at one time. Taft and Carter became teachers or professors after they left office.

125. George Washington.

126. James Madison, who is known as "The Father of the Constitution."

127. John F. Kennedy.

128. James Monroe, when he defeated Rufus King in the 1816 election! Tricky, eh?

129. Theodore Roosevelt.

130. Ulysses S. Grant, who, in 1872, defeated Victoria Woodhull, in addition to Democrat Horace Greeley.

131. Millard Fillmore.

132. Abraham Lincoln. In 1849, he invented a flotation device for "buoying vessels over shoals." This invention was impractical and never put to use.

133. James A. Garfield, when he campaigned in the 1880 election.

134. Herbert Hoover.

135. Franklin Pierce, who retained all seven cabinet members until he completed his term on March 3, 1857.

136. Herbert Hoover, living 31 years after his Presidency.

137. Martin Van Buren.

138. John Tyler (his second wife).

139. Ulysses S. Grant, whose tomb is located on Riverside Drive.

140. Franklin Pierce, born on November 23, 1804. Millard Fillmore was born in 1800, but many historians consider this the last year of the 18th century.

141. John Tyler, but Whigs and Democrats united to defeat the measure.

142. I just told you! John Tyler, when Congress overrode his veto of a naval bill on March 3, 1844, Tyler's last full day in office.

143. Theodore Roosevelt, while on an expedition to the Amazon. His small party of adventurers reached the point of starvation and subsisted on monkey meat. The former President developed an abscess and a high fever and told the men with him he wanted to die. After a few hours of coaxing, Teddy was brought to his senses and the group found their way out of the tropics.

144. Lyndon Johnson, sworn in by Sarah Hughes aboard a plane in Dallas, Texas, in 1963.

145. James Garfield, Benjamin Harrison, William McKinley, and Warren Harding, all Republicans from Ohio.

146. William Howard Taft, who eventually became Chief Justice during Harding's administration. He told President Theodore Roosevelt he wanted to stay with his "little brown brothers" in the Philippines where he served as governor.

147. Elizabeth Monroe. She became very

popular in France as her husband served as the American Minister during the 1790's.

148. Louisa Catherine Johnson Adams, wife of John Quincy Adams. Though her father was an American, she was born in London in 1775 to an English mother.

149. Abigail Fillmore, who was a school teacher.

150. Harriet Lane served for her uncle James Buchanan, our only bachelor President.

151. Mrs. Ellen Wilson, the President's first wife.

152. Helen Taft.

153. Abigail Fillmore attended Franklin Pierce's inauguration on a cold, wind-swept day and caught a cold which developed into pneumonia. She died that same month in the nation's capital.

154. Edith Galt Wilson, Woodrow Wilson's second wife. She played a significant role during her husband's second term while he was disabled by a stroke.

155. Frances Folsom Cleveland, who became a White House bride at age 21. Cleveland's sister was the official hostess the first 15 months of his first term.

156. Actually it was two wives. Sarah Polk and Lucy Hayes, dubbed "Lemonade Lucy" by the press. One guest at the White House in 1878 said the water flowed like wine!

157. Sarah Polk.

158. Helen Herron Taft.

159. Because of his sudden death in San Francisco in 1923 and the fact that there was no autopsy allowed, speculation is that President Warren G. Harding may have been poisoned by his wife, Florence. Though rumors persist there was foul play, they are unfounded. She was, however, well aware of the impending scandals about to break. Known as the "Duchess," she and Harding's private nurse were the last to see him alive.

160. Jacqueline Bouvier Kennedy.

161. Pat Nixon.

162. Eleanor Roosevelt.

163. Edith Wilson, the President's second wife.

164. Mamie Eisenhower. Mary Todd Lincoln was also known as a "big spender" on clothing, once buying 500 pairs of gloves, only to wear a couple of pairs.

165. Harry Truman, referring to Bess.

166. Pat Nixon.

167. Shan.

168. Abraham Lincoln.

169. George Washington, who vetoed only two bills during his eight years as President.

170. The ex-President was Benjamin Harrison, who was at the time a guest lecturer at Stanford University in 1894. The young student manager was the future 31st President, Herbert Hoover.

171. Rosalynn Smith Carter gave birth to Amy just two months after her 40th birthday.

172. Theodore Roosevelt.

173. Dwight Eisenhower, who lived in Gettysburg, Pennsylvania.

174. Pat Nixon.

175. It was written in the same hotel room where Warren G. Harding died in San Francisco about a decade before.

176. Andrew Jackson.

177. Ronald Reagan, born on February 6, 1911, in Tampico, Illinois.

178. Dwight Eisenhower did it in February of 1968, seven years after leaving office.

179. Richard Nixon.

180. Franklin D. Roosevelt did this immediately following the attack on Pearl Harbor on December 7, 1941.

181. George Washington.

182. The Spirit of '76.

183. Abraham Lincoln.

184. Abraham Lincoln in Springfield, Il-

linois, and Benjamin Harrison in Indianapolis, Indiana.

185. This pertained to Harry Truman's architectural designs to change the South Portico entrance of the White House, which included adding a balcony. When Gilmore Clark, chairman of the Fine Arts Commission which approved such projects, refused the President's plans, Truman fired him and then had his balcony installed.

186. Jimmy and Rosalynn Carter.

187. Thomas Jefferson. Some sources say that the "tom" in tomato comes from the multi-talented Virginian.

188. Dolley Madison, during Jefferson's two terms. Jefferson and his Vice President, Aaron Burr, were both widowers, and it fell upon Mrs. Madison, wife of the Secretary of State at the time, to serve as hostess.

189. The other quote was "Always do right. This will gratify some people and astonish the rest." This quote came from another Missourian, Mark Twain.

190. John Tyler. The "Tyler-grippe" swept the nation in 1841-1842.

191. James K. Polk.

192. Jimmy Carter.

193. Harry Truman.

194. Andrew Jackson.

195. Woodrow Wilson, who is buried in the District of Columbia. Taft and Kennedy are buried in Arlington, Virginia.

196. William H. Taft and Gerald Ford (law school).

197. William McKinley.

198. Chester Arthur.

199. New Hampshire (White Mountains).

200. John Adams. John Kennedy and Lyndon Johnson were also skinny dippers, using the White House pool.

Hidden Word Answers

1-Nixon, 2-Hayes, 3-Taylor, 4-Harding, 5-Harrison, 6-Arthur, 7-Grant, 8-Truman, 9-Cleveland, 10-Hoover, 11-Ford, 12-Jackson, 13-Taft, 14-Garfield, 15-Adams, 16-Kennedy, 17-Carter, 18-Reagan, 19-Pierce, 20-Johnson.

Answers to Matching

Nicknames: 1-C, 2-H, 3-I, 4-J, 5-K, 6-A, 7-D, 8-G, 9-L, 10-F, 11-E, 12-B.

Coins: 1-E, 2-C, 3-D, 4-A, 5-B, 6-F.

Horses: 1-D, 2-A, 3-B, 4-C, 5-E.

Scandals: 1-C, 2-A, 3-C or D (preceded Garfield's Presidency), 4-F, 5-E, 6-B.

More nicknames: 1-B, 2-E, 3-D, 4-A, 5-C.

Quotes: 1. B—FDR said that in 1940.
2. E—said to colleagues in 1912.
3. A—as a Congressman in 1847.
4. D—at a banquet for John C. Calhoun in 1832.
5. C—on television in 1973.
6. H—stated publicly while President.
7. G—made to friends while President.

8. F—comment made to advisers while President.

Dogs: 1-E, 2-H, 3-D, 4-I, 5-F, 6-A, 7-C, 8-G, 9-B, 10-J.

Yachts: 1-D, 2-C, 3-E, 4-A, 5-B.

Signatures:

A-3 James K. Polk
B-5 Grover Cleveland
C-6 Warren G. Harding
D-7 John F. Kennedy
E-2 William Henry Harrison
F-9 Lyndon B. Johnson
G-4 Ulysses S. Grant
H-1 George Washington
I-8 Thomas Jefferson

Bibliography

Adams, James Truslow, *The Epic of America*, Triangle Books, New York, 1941.

Adler, Bill, *The Washington Wits*, Macmillan Publishing Co., New York, 1967.

Agel, Jerome, *America at Random: Q & A*, Arbor House, New York, 1983.

Allen, Robert S. and Shannon, William V., *The Truman Merry-Go-Round*, Vanguard Press, New York, 1950.

Andrist, Ralph K., ed., *George Washington: A Biography in His Own Words*, Newsweek, New York, 1972.

Angle, Paul M. ed., *The Lincoln Reader*, Rutgers University Press, New Brunswick, New Jersey, 1947.

Asimov, Isaac, *Isaac Asimov's Book of Facts*, Bell Publishing Co., New York, 1979.

Bartlett, John, *Bartlett's Familiar Quotations*, Little, Brown and Co., Boston, 1968.

Boller, Paul F. Jr., *Presidential Anecdotes*, Penguin Books, New York, 1981.

Botkin, B.A. ed., *A Treasury of American Anecdotes*, Bonanza Books, New York, 1967.

Boyd, L.M., *Boyd's Book of Odd Facts*, Signet, New York, 1979.

Caro, Robert A., *The Years of Lyndon Johnson: The Path to Power*, Alfred A. Knopf, New York, 1982.

Carter, Jimmy, *Keeping Faith,* Bantam Books, New York, 1982.

Cavanah, Frances, *Meet the Presidents,* Macrae Smith Co., Philadelphia, 1962.

Cooke, Alistair, *America,* Alfred A. Knopf, Inc., New York, 1974.

Dempsey, Jack, *Dempsey,* Harper and Row, New York, 1977.

Eisenhower, Dwight D., *Waging Peace,* Doubleday, Garden City, New York, 1965.

Ford, Betty, *The Times of My Life,* Harper and Row, New York, 1972.

Frank, Sid, *The Presidents: Tidbits and Trivia,* Hammond, Inc., Maplewood, New Jersey, 1977.

Freidel, Frank, *Our Country's Presidents,* National Geographic Society, Washington, D.C. 1979.

Furnas, J.C., *The Americans,* G.P. Putnam's Sons, New York, 1969.

Goulder, Grace, *This is Ohio,* The World Publishing Co., Cleveland, Ohio, 1965.

Graff, Robert D. and Ginna, Robert E., *FDR,* Harper and Row, New York, 1963.

Hess, Stephen, *Organizing the Presidency,* Brookings Institution, Washington, D.C. 1976.

Hoff, Rhoda, *They Grew to be President,* Doubleday and Co., Inc., Garden City, New York, 1971.

Howe, George Frederick, *Chester A. Arthur,* Frederick Ungar Publishing Co., New York, 1957.

Johnson, Lyndon Baines, *The Vantage Point: Perspectives of the Presidency 1963-1969,* Holt, Rinehart and Winston, New York, 1971.

Kane, Joseph Nathan, *Facts About The Presidents,* H.W. Wilson Co., New York, 1964.

Kennan, George F., *Memoirs: 1925-1950,* Little, Brown and Co., Boston, 1967.

Ketchum, Richard M., *Faces from the Past,* American Heritage Press, New York, 1970.

Kittler, Glenn D., *Hail to the Chief,* Chilton Book Co., Philadelphia, 1965.

Klapthor, Margaret Brown and The White House Historical Assn., *The First Ladies,* Washington, D.C. 1975.

Knepper, George, *An Ohio Portrait,* Ohio Historical Society, Columbus, Ohio, 1976.

Krock, Arthur, *Memoirs,* Funk and Wagnalls, New York, 1968.

Kunhardt, Dorothy Meserve and Kunhardt, Philip B., *Twenty Days,* Castle Books, New York, 1965.

Lengyel, Cornel Adam, *Presidents of the United States,* Golden Press, New York, 1964.

Lorant, Stefan, *Lincoln: A Picture Story of His Life,* Bonanza Books, New York, 1969.

Lorant, Stefan, *The Glorious Burden,* Authors Edition, Inc., Lenox, Mass., 1976.

Louis, David, *2201 Fascinating Facts,* Greenwich House, New York, 1983.

McConnell, Jane and Burt, *Our First Ladies,* Thomas Y. Crowell, New York, 1969.

McConnell, Jane and Burt, *Presidents of the United States,* Thomas Y. Crowell Co., New York, 1965.

McElroy, Richard L., *The Best of Baseball Trivia,* Western Reserve Magazine Press, Garrettsville, Ohio, 1981.

McFeely, William S., *Grant,* W.W. Norton and Co., New York, 1981.

Manchester, William, *The Death of a President,* Harper and Row, New York, 1967.

Melick, Arden Davis, *Wives of the Presidents,* Hammond, Inc., Maplewood, New Jersey, 1972.

Miers, Earl S., *America and Its Presidents,* Grosset and Dunlap, New York, 1964.

Mollenhoff, Clark R., *Game Plan for Disaster: An Ombudsman's Report on the Nixon Years,* W.W. Norton and Co., Inc., New York, 1976.

Moore, Bernard and Ehrlich, Richard, ed., *Mothers: 100 Mothers of The Famous And The Infamous,* Paddington Press Ltd., New York, 1976.

Morgan, James, *Our Presidents,* The Macmillan Co., New York, 1969.

Morin, Relman, *Dwight D. Eisenhower—A Gauge of Greatness,* The Associated Press, 1969.

Morris, Edmund, *The Rise of Theodore Roosevelt,* Coward, McCann and Geoghan, Inc., New York, 1979.

Peskin, Allan, *Garfield,* Kent State University Press, Kent, Ohio, 1978.

Peterson, Merrill D., ed., *James Madison: A Biography in His Own Words,* Newsweek, New York, 1974.

Reeves, Richard, *A Ford, Not A Lincoln,* Harcourt Brace Jovanovich, New York, 1975.

Robertson, Patrick, *The Book of Firsts,* Bramhall House, New York, 1974.

Russell, Francis, *The Shadow Of Blooming Grove: Warren G. Harding in His Times,* McGraw-Hill Publishing Co., New York, 1968.

Schachner, Nathan, *Thomas Jefferson: A Biography,* Thomas Yoseloff, Publisher, New York, 1957.

Shenkman, Richard and Reiger, Kurt, *One-Night Stands with American History,* Quill, New York, 1982.

Shepherd, Jack, *The Adams Chronicles,* Little, Brown and Co., Boston, 1975.

Shor, Frank, Breeden, Robert and The White House Historical Assn., *The Presidents of the United States of America,* Washington, D.C. 1975.

Smith, Bessie White, *The Boyhoods of the Presidents,* Lothrop, Lee and Shepard Co., Boston, 1929.

Smith, Don, *Peculiarities of the Presidents,* Wilkinson Press, Van Wert, Ohio, 1946.

Smith, Gene, *When The Cheering Stopped,* William Morrow and Co., New York, 1964.

Smith, Page, *The Nation Comes of Age,* McGraw-Hill Book Co., New York, 1981.

Smith, Page, *Trial By Fire,* McGraw-Hill Book Co., New York, 1982.

Truman, Margaret, *Harry S. Truman,* William Morrow and Co., New York, 1972.

Wallace, Amy, Wallechinsky, David, and Wallace, Irving, *The Book of Lists #3,* William Morrow and Co., New York, 1983.

Weichmann, Louis J., *A True History of the Assassination of Abraham Lincoln and the Conspiracy of 1865,* Alfred A. Knopf, Inc., New York, 1975.

West, J.B., *Upstairs at the White House,* Coward, McCann and Geoghegan, New York, 1973.

Worth, Fred L., *The Complete Unabridged Super Trivia Encyclopedia,* Brooke House, Los Angeles, 1977.

The following newspapers and magazines were also used: *The Akron Beacon Journal, The Canton Repository, The Cleveland Plain Dealer, The Buckeye Flyer Magazine, Western Reserve Magazine, The Hayes Historical Journal, American Heritage Magazine, Family Weekly, Saturday Evening Post,* and *Ohio Cues Magazine.*